FEAR

THE FRIEND OF EXCEPTIONAL PEOPLE

Geoff Thompson

SUMMERSDALE

First published 1995.

Reprinted 1995, 1996 (twice), 1997, 1998, 1999

Summersdale Publishers Ltd
46 West Street
Chichester
West Sussex
PO19 1RP
United Kingdom

www.summersdale.com

Printed and bound by Cox & Wyman Ltd, Reading, Berks.

ISBN 1 84024 091 1

The chemicals released from the adrenal gland are not adrenalin, though they are commonly referred to as adrenalin. Throughout the book I have called these chemicals adrenalin for the sake of simplicity.

The Ground Fighting Series (videos):

Vol. One   – Pins, the Bedrock
Vol. Two   – Escapes
Vol. Three   – Chokes and Strangles
Vol. Four   – Arm Bars and Joint Locks
Vol. Five   – Fighting From Your Back
Vol. Six   – Fighting From Neutral Knees

Advanced Ground Fighting Vols. 1-3
Pavement Arena Part 1
Pavement Arena Part 2   – The Protection Pyramid
Pavement Arena Part 3   – Grappling, The Last Resort
Pavement Arena Part 4   – Fit To Fight

About the Author:

Geoff Thompson has written over 20 published books and is known world wide for his autobiographical books *Watch My back, Bouncer* and *On The Door*, about his nine years working as a night club doorman. He holds the rank of 5th Dan black belt in Japanese karate, 1st Dan in Judo and is also qualified to senior instructor level in various other forms of wrestling and martial arts. He has several scripts for stage, screen and TV in development with Destiny Films.

He has published several articles for GQ magazine, and has also been featured in *FHM*, *Maxim*, *Arena*, *Front* and *Loaded* magazines, and has been featured many times on mainstream TV.

Geoff is currently a contributing editor for *Men's Fitness* magazine and self defence columnist for *Front*.

Contents

INTRODUCTION

The Jonah complex (a fear of success)

We are generally afraid to become that which we can glimpse in our most perfect moments, under the most perfect conditions, under conditions of greatest courage, we enjoy and even thrill to the god-like possibilities we see in ourselves at such peak moments, and yet, simultaneously, shiver with weakness, awe and fear before the same possibilities. **Abraham Moslow**.

Working one's way through a life that is fraught with intangible confrontation, in an adrenal loaded body that was better designed for conflicts of the tangible kind, fight or flight, it is a small wonder that most people do go to their graves with their best songs still in them. For the adrenal syndrome, that was better suited to the mortal conflict of fighting or escaping the sabre toothed tiger, is lost in a decade where confrontation may be a board room meeting, high mortgage rates or a row with the spouse.

Tangible confrontation on a base level, where the adrenal rush adds speed, power and anaesthesia to response, has been succeeded by confrontations of a rather translucent nature, a run in with the boss or perhaps a business decision. In the latter scenarios adrenalin is released but not utilised because neither fight nor flight is an option. It would be unreasonable and anti-social (though often damned tempting) to strike a vindictive boss and unwise (though very common) to run away from confrontations in the home. So one often finds oneself infused with unrecognised and un-utilised adrenalin. The subsequent inner pressure eventually explodes like the cork of a shaken Champagne bottle, usually, unexpectedly and often without warning or provocation, into other aspects of our lives.

Concurrently the reasoning process, misreading the feeling of adrenalin for fear, builds a subconscious periphery that imprisons the part of us that wants to achieve. Fear is what keeps people ordinary.

It is said that knowledge dispels fear. Have a good look around you, also have a good look at yourself. How many people do you know who are truly happy with their lot? Society is full of under achievers, and not because we lack potential nor courage, rather we lack an understanding of our own bodily reactions to confrontation. Because of this, adrenalin often catalyses panic, forcing a possible abortion of plans to change, expand, explore etc for fear of consequence or often for fear of fear itself.

25 centuries ago general Sun Tzu said 'if you know your enemy and know yourself you need not fear the outcome of a hundred battles'. Knowing yourself is understanding that the enemy is within and that society is the battle field.

As Ian Botham said, 'life is not a rehearsal' - we have one chance to do something and this is it. Most people are living lives that they don't want to live. Why? Because they are imprisoned in a 'safe bet' comfort parameter they dare not exit for fear of failure, success, change, risk, ridicule or whatever. They dream of better jobs, happier relationships, nicer cars, of success and fulfilment but those ideals are seldom realised because lying ominously between fancy and fact is FEAR.

The blame for failure is frequently off-loaded with the *excuse syndrome*. 'If it wasn't for **************** I could really do something with my life.'

Most of us sit in the driveway of life watching it go by, too scared to pull out into the traffic, frightened to use fuel, and afraid in case we crash. Many have the dynamite needed to explode into an adventurous life but few the match of courage and understanding to light the fuse.

What most fail to realise is that whether you are facing a big business deal, a showdown with the boss or a couple of muggers up an entry you will feel fear. It is as much its unexpectedness as the feeling itself that turns men to mice.

When life presents us with a confrontation of any kind we will feel fear, granted its manifestation carries many disguises with varying degrees of intensity. Nevertheless, it will be present.

The purpose of this book is to help break down the prison walls by educating people in the histrionics of fear. How to recognise, understand and subsequently control and/or employ it as an ally.

This is not a book about phobias, though the symptoms and remedies herein are parallelled with those of the phobic condition. When dealing with fear at most levels the response of exposure therapy is the same. Systematically confronting a fear until desensitization occurs.

Fear never goes away!

I learned very early on in my practice that whilst we can lose a fear of a certain thing or situation we will never get rid of fear completely, it will always be there whilst we continue to expand. Rather we learn to recognise and control fear deeming it a powerful tool that will aid us in our response to confrontation.

The intent of this book is to allow people to see themselves from the inside out so that panic is replaced by understanding and discomfort by relief.

The world is your Oyster, it is only you who hold yourself back.

CHAPTER ONE

WHAT IS FEAR?

The coward and the hero both feel the same feelings, (of fear) the only difference between the two is that the hero handles the feelings and the coward does not. Cus Damatio (trainer to Mike Tyson)

What is it? What is fear? How can one define it? The English dictionary informs us that fear is:
An unpleasant, often strong emotion caused by anticipation or awareness of danger.

In layman's terms when the brain senses danger it triggers adrenalin, this being a human turbo charge, brought on by awareness/anticipation to aid *fight or flight*. This unpleasant, strong emotion often causes terror immobilisation, or the freeze syndrome in the recipient.

Adrenalin is a little like *fuel injection* or *turbo drive* in a sports car, action, the metaphoric accelerator.

The car: by engaging the clutch, and pressing the accelerator you will utilise the *turbo*, and the car will move at speed. However, if you sit at the traffic lights pressing your foot on the accelerator without engaging the clutch, there will be no movement and fuel will be wasted.

The human: by engaging *action* (fight/flight) you will utilise the *turbo drive* of adrenalin, and trigger spontaneous response.

However, if *action* is not engaged and panic sets in, energy will be utilised negatively.

Body accelerators

Positive body accelerator
Your positive body accelerator is action. When you act (engage the clutch), ie. confront your fear, adrenalin is utilised positively, adding vigour to your response.

Negative body accelerator
Your negative body accelerator is *panic*, caused when the reasoning process mistakes adrenalin for fear. Adrenalin is utilised negatively, leaving the recipient drained of energy and often frozen in the face of ensuing danger.

If you find yourself in a confrontational situation and do not or cannot *act*, the adrenalin will be gobbled up by increasing panic, this dissipating your turbo blast needlessly and fruitlessly. Like the car, you will be pressing the accelerator without engaging the clutch. Nothing is gained and all is lost.

In the gap between confrontation and action adrenalin can be controlled with deep breathing and knowledge, and the look of fear hidden with *the duck syndrome* (detailed later).

Through my own search and experimentation I have learned that the explosion inside the stomach that so many people struggle with and that causes the infamous *freeze* syndrome which begets defeat is adrenalin.

In primeval days when mankind had to fight to live and eat, the feeling of fear was an every day occurrence that would have felt as natural and as common as eating or drinking. In today's society, where confrontation is less tangible, the act of fighting or running for our lives is no longer a part of every day living, so when a situation arises that causes the adrenalin to flow, and because we are so unfamiliar with it (unlike our pre-historic ancestors) we, naturally, neither welcome, use or like it (we panic). Psychologists call it the *fight or flight* syndrome. In moments of danger/confrontation the body releases chemicals from the adrenal gland that hits and goes through the blood-stream like a speeding train, preparing the body for *fight or flight*, deeming it stronger, faster and partially, sometimes completely, anaesthetised to pain. The more demanding the situation the bigger the build-up and adrenalin release, the bigger the release the better the performance (run, fight), but by the same count, the bigger the build-up and release, the harder it is to control.

Subsequently, because the adrenalin often lies un-utilised in the body it builds up, like a pressure cooker, and explodes in other aspects of our lives, ie. in the car, road-rage, or in the home, shouting at the wife/husband/children etc.

Adrenalin is released into the body in several ways. I will take them in turn.

Think-confrontation fear
When you anticipate confrontation the body releases adrenalin slowly and often over a long period. The slow release is not so intense as the fast release but, due to its longevity, it can wear and corrode the recipient. Things like anticipation of having to talk in public, an exam, a big sales meeting, a forthcoming karate competition, a planned confrontation with the husband/wife/neighbour/boss etc. will cause slow release often up to months before the expected confrontation.

Pre/post-confrontation fear
When one anticipates the consequence of confrontation, negative or positive, before it even happens, the fear of that

consequence, failure, success, humiliation etc. often forces the recipient to abort.

Pre-confrontation fear

Psychologists like to call this *adrenal dump*, the body guards list it as *the WOW factor*. The fast release occurs when anticipation is not present, or a situation escalates unexpectedly fast, causing adrenal dump, this feeling is often so intense that the recipient freezes in the face of confrontation, the reasoning process mistaking it for sheer terror. This the most devastating of the three.

Adrenal dump often occurs when a confrontation arises that one was not ready or prepared for, usually the same scenarios as those that cause slow release but with no anticipation. Perhaps you are in a meeting at work and are unexpectedly asked to address those present without any preparation or you are confronted, again without warning, by your boss/ neighbour/partner or an attacker etc.

Secondary adrenalin

Before, during or after a confrontation something may happen that you hadn't counted on, the brain sensing this unpreparedness gives the body a second kick of adrenalin that is nearly always misread for fear.

In-confrontation fear

During confrontation you stumble and things are not going to plan, the brain again sensing a danger offers a second kick of a adrenalin to help you out. This offering is misread for fear and panic ensues.

Post-confrontation fear - *Aftermath*.

After confrontation, whether successful or not, the body often secretes slow releases of adrenalin in anticipation of consequence. In attack situations consequence may be police involvement, revenge attacks etc. In business, the consequence may be the result of a decision that could bankrupt your company.

Adrenal Combo
Those working/living in a stress related environment, the stock exchange, business, security etc. may experience a combination (combo) of the latter. There is slow release because they anticipate confrontation, adrenal dump when situations unexpectedly occur in their environment and aftermath, in relation to situations that have already happened.

The duck syndrome
In many aspects of confrontation, certainly business and combat, it can be to the recipient's detriment to show that he is suffering the ills of fear, this often being construed as a weak link. In such circumstances it would be wise to hide the effects of adrenalin. Even in nature a dog will attack when he senses fear, the same can be said in all walks of life from selling to combat.

A duck will appear to glide through the water with grace and elegance. Under the water his little webbed feet will be going like the clappers. When you understand and can control the adrenal flow it is possible to hide adrenal reaction ('going like the clappers') by appearing unmoved and calm. This deceives those around you into believing that you are not scared. As an old sage once said, 'When ignorance is mutual, confidence is king.'

As I mentioned before, recognising the feeling of fear and understanding its mechanics will help to minimise its shock impetus.

These are the possible, natural bodily reactions to adrenalin:

Pre fight shakes
Your legs, and possibly other limbs, may shake uncontrollably.

Dry mouth
Your mouth may become dry and pasty.

Voice quiver
Your voice may acquire a nervous and audible tremor.

Tunnel vision
On the positive side tunnel vision enhances visual concentration.
Its negative by-product is blinkering of peripheral vision.

Sweaty palms and forehead
The palms of the hands and forehead often sweat profusely.

Nausea
Adrenalin may cause vomiting, or the feeling of vomiting.

Bowel loosening
The recipient may experience constant urges to use the toilet.

'Yellow' fever
Adrenalin, certainly adrenal dump, evokes feelings of
helplessness and abject terror. Fear of confrontation may bring
on an extreme feeling of depression and foreboding. Tears may
also occur.

Time distortion
Many reported that confrontation seemed to last an eternity,
when in reality it may have only lasted a few minutes. During
confrontation time can appear to stand still, one minute often
feeling like one hour. Paradoxically, in retrospect, many have
said, 'It all happened so fast'. When interviewing James, the
victim of an unsolicited assault, he initially told me that he
was attacked without warning. After talking to him at some

length it turned out that, between first seeing his attackers and the attack itself, there was a time lapse of 11 seconds, this being lost to time distortion.

Restless nights
Many suffer from restless nights when experiencing slow release and aftermath.

No appetite
Appetite tends to lessen, often resulting in weight loss, especially with slow release and aftermath.

Increased heart rate
Due to the turbo drive of adrenalin the heart rate often increases to what the recipient may feel is an abnormal level, some may even experience chest pains as a result of tenseness in the pectoral region.

Depression
As a result of all the inner turmoil brought on by anticipation depression often occurs.

These are not the only bodily reactions to adrenalin, though they are certainly the main ones. Other reactions may occur as a direct result of confrontation.

All of the forgoing feelings are usual. Accept and ignore them whenever possible, they are all part and parcel of adrenal reaction and, though unpleasant, quite natural. The feelings cannot hurt or harm you and they do lessen in intensity as you become more exposed to them.

The only thing we have to fear is fear itself.
Franklin D Roosevelt.

CHAPTER TWO

THE FIRST STEP

Even a journey of one thousand miles begins with a first step. The first step with fear is self-honesty. Many people never overcome their fears because they are afraid to admit them. Possibly they are embarrassed, even ashamed to admit their supposed failings, perhaps believing that others may think them weak for harbouring such fears. In reality it is truly a strong person who can be honest with themselves: I know, I spent years lying to myself, and being very unhappy as a direct result. Even an alcoholic cannot begin treatment until he first admits that he is an alcoholic.

The feeling of fear is as natural as the feelings of hunger and thirst and of wanting to use the toilet. I never met anyone that felt embarrassed or ashamed because they felt hungry, or thirsty or because they needed to use the loo.

I have worked and met with many people who told me that they felt no fear. They all turned out to be either very misguided or, as it turned out, blatant liars.

Saying that you don't feel fear is the same as saying that you don't feel hunger, thirst, love or hate. Everyone feels emotion, fear being one of the most powerful and prime-evil of those emotions.

Fear is triggered by anticipation of confrontation and is nature's way of helping us to survive life or death situations. Of course confrontation is no longer the one dimensional fight/flight scenario it was in by-gone years. If you were attacked by a sabre toothed tiger you had two options. Your first option was, when possible, always flight, when this was not an option it was fight for your life. Confrontation in the 20th century is rather more perplexing and our cosmopolitan society a complicated paradox where, at once, both fight and flight are largely unacceptable. We are taught from primary school level that fighting is wrong whilst at the same time we are seen as cowards if we do not fight back against our adversaries.

Our body and mind are constantly at a moral loggerhead. Physical instinct tells us to run or fight for survival, morality and contemporary peer pressure says 'don't fight!' whilst at the same time it reminds us to 'stand up for yourself'. Even the law punishes us for our instinct, even when we are only defending ourselves or our loved ones.

The brain, it would seem, on a subconscious level, cannot distinguish between varying kinds of confrontation. If we anticipate a tangible confrontation, where the possible outcome may be a fight, the brain triggers adrenalin to aid response. If we anticipate an intangible confrontation, where there is no possibility of a physical outcome, ie a school exam, driving test, a speech, a show down with the boss etc. the brain still releases adrenalin to aid response, and often, due to the nature of the confrontation, the adrenalin is not utilised and lies dormant in the body only to be released when someone cuts you up in the car or your child innocently spills a juice drink on the carpet.

Admitting your fears is often very a personal issue, perhaps not something that you would want to tell the whole world about. That's O.K. Telling others is not always important, self-honesty, though, is.

Often people will say, 'I'm not afraid of it (whatever it may be) I just don't want to do it'.

As a younger person I would always convince myself that 'I'm not afraid of Karate competitions, I'm just not interested in competing'. If that was the case it would have been fine. In reality I found even the thought of competing nerve-wracking and would experience slow release adrenalin up to a couple of months before the contest. This long term anticipation would cause me sleepless nights and lessen my appetite. Lack of good food and sleep caused weight loss and depression. All of a sudden I was on a downward spiral, anticipation triggering many negative bodily reactions. The fact that I wasn't sleeping and eating would make me feel worse because, as I saw it, if I wasn't sleeping and eating then I must really have a problem. The lack of food and sleep would also make me very tired, being constantly tired lowered my defences leaving me at the mercy of the Voice, my inner opponent, who constantly told me how weak I was and how I couldn't handle it (the situation). Eventually I would get so down about the whole thing that I would ring up my instructor and make up some silly excuse as to why I couldn't enter the competition (I will talk more about the inner opponent in a later chapter).

This scenario is probably familiar to many: how often have you avoided certain scenarios due to the discomfort of anticipation and then made up an excuse to cover your avoidance?

Admitting your fears is the first and foremost step in overcoming fear. Without self honesty you are not even on the first rung of the ladder, neither will you ever be if you can't be honest with yourself.

It is also important not to kid yourself, 'When I feel a little better about myself I'll do it' (confront your fear). 'When I'm a little fitter I'll enter a contest.' 'When I've got a little more money in the bank I'll start my own business.' And when you have enough money in the bank, 'I don't feel right yet, as soon as I do I'll go out on my own.'

There will always be a good excuse not to confront, always a good reason not to start, stop, leave, fight etc. It is worth remembering that 'it will be hard'. If it was easy everyone would be a black belt in karate, a successful businessman, a confident person, have a great physique, hold a top job, drive the dream car and live with the perfect partner.

If you want success, in whatever form that may take, NOW is the time to start, not tomorrow, not next week, not on New Year's Day, now. Any delay always hints to me of a lack of commitment. Whoever you want to be, wherever you want to go, whatever you want to achieve can be done, but only you can do it. I can't give it to you, neither can anyone else. What I can do, however, is show you the way, so as to make the journey a little easier.

CHAPTER THREE

A FEW HOME TRUTHS

Before engaging a challenge, before setting out on any journey it is best to make plans, as Sun Tzu said,
If you know the time and place of the attack you can plan your defence from a hundred miles away.

There will be difficult times along the way, understanding this at the onset will lessen the shock impetus of any setbacks. The journey itself is where the real learning takes place. Here are a few truths to be remembered:

1) *As long as you continue to learn and grow, fear will never go away.*
En route you will overcome many different fears, these will bring a higher self esteem and desensitisation to adrenalin. However, each time you approach a new situation at higher levels and each time you find yourself in unfamiliar circumstances you will again feel fear. Each new and subsequent fear will be more easily defeated, the techniques and confidence you have learned en route will serve you in good stead when confronting fresh fears.

2) *The only way to overcome the fear of doing something is to go out and do it.*
You can sit in the classroom all day long talking about different aspects of your particular fear and how you're going to overcome them, what a great life you will have thereafter and the wonderful things that you want to achieve, but, at the end of the day you will not learn to swim until you immerse yourself in the water. In other words, the only way to practice is to confront. No confrontation, no desensitisation. There are those

who stay up all night dreaming about it and there are those who stay up all night doing it.

Don't talk the talk when you can walk the walk.

Having said that I have found that knowledge itself sometimes dispels fear to such an extent that confrontation is no longer a necessity. The more you understand and can learn about your particular fear the better, if it doesn't dispel it completely it will, at least, make it easier to confront. As they say 'you cannot destroy what you cannot create'.

3) *The only way you are going to feel better and get stronger is to go out and do it.*
Everywhere I go I am confronted by people who are going to do this and going to do that, every time I'm in the pub I'm told by beer guzzlers about great plans that are going to be realised, starting first thing tomorrow/next week/next year. Dreams that evaporate with soberness. Ironically a lot of these 'talkers' really do have the potential to realise all of their dreams if only they had the courage and enlightenment of conviction. I know many people in my own life who have bags of potential but, for whatever reasons, they fail to utilise any of it and settle instead for the safe bet life of mediocrity.

4) *Everyone feels fear, especially in unfamiliar territory.*
As a young person, frightened by my own shadow, I always felt that I was the only one that felt 'this scared'. This thought never ceased to spiral me down into ever increasing misery. The greatest revelation for me was the fact that everyone felt the same in confrontational circumstances, though few of the people I spoke to in the early days would admit it. Do as I did and take great solace in the fact that 'we all feel the same'. Some of the most successful people in the world started out as mentally weak and fearful people.

One of my friends, an S.A.S. soldier, a veteran of the Iranian Embassy siege, spent the first year of his army life as a frightened, bullied 16 year old. I asked him, out of all the life threatening situations that he found himself in, which was the hardest to overcome. You may find it surprising to hear that, in his opinion, the bravest thing that he ever did was confront a bully when he was 16 years old, probably because it was his first step into the fear syndrome. Using this early lesson as a catalyst he later joined the S.A.S. and became one of the world's elite soldiers facing death on a daily basis.

5) *It gets easier.*
The hardest step is often the first step. The first step is the decision to start, the decision not to take second place, the decision to fight back. Once you have made that decision you are half way there. The beauty of it all is, once you have gotten started and get a few successes under your belt you really start to enjoy the challenge. It is a little like the guys on the world's strongest man contest pulling trucks. Getting the truck started is a real toil, but once they build momentum it becomes easier and easier. It is a lot easier to keep momentum than to start it.

6) *Living with fear is probably more painful that confronting fear.*
I personally found that living with my fears was a lot more painful than actually confronting them. And, certainly when living with fear, your life and potential is severely restricted whereas in confronting fear you are constantly expanding your life and potential. When I was living under the dominion of my fears I felt almost imprisoned, the decision to confront and overcome them was like the cell doors opening.

When I was scared and doing nothing about it my life seemed empty and limited by the walls of those fears, when I went into action with a plan of attack my life suddenly became exiting and prosperous. The more I got into it the more I realised that there was nothing I could not do if you really wanted to.

Whatever the mind of man can conceive he can achieve.

This short extract is taken from my autobiographical book *Watch My Back* and tells a little of my early journey.

All my early life, certainly from the age of eleven, I was plagued by a fear of fighting and confrontations. My mind was weak and constantly under attack from fears too powerful to defend against. Doubtless I was not on my own in this respect, but at the time I felt I was, so I could take no solace in the former. What I found to my distaste was not 'being scared' but the thought of having to live under its dominion for the rest of my life.

Many's the time I found myself sneaking out of the school's back entrance to avoid my would-be antagonists waiting for me at the front, and running off to the sanctuary of short-sightedness and ignorance only to wake up the next morning with fear and worry ever growing at the thought of having to go back to school and face 'the enemy' again, often having to go under the protective wing of my dad.

I vividly remember one Christmas morning sitting in my bedroom and crying, worrying about going back to school in two weeks' time, and the misery that would then ensue, and my elder brother coming in and asking me what was wrong. I shrugged my shoulders, too ashamed to admit my weakness. My whole childhood was marred by such incidents: these sad, scared, worried feelings came and went at will - I was at the mercy of my own mind.

In later years, and through my searching and experimenting, I learned that the explosion inside my stomach that I had once took for sheer terror and had struggled so long with was the adrenalin build up, or the fight or flight syndrome, a chemical release from the adrenal gland that hits and goes through the blood stream like a speeding tube train, preparing the body for fight or flight. It makes you temporarily stronger and faster and partially anaesthetises you from pain. The more dangerous the situation, the bigger the build up and adrenalin release; the bigger the release the better you perform. But by the same count the bigger the build-up and release the harder it is to control, ie. the easier it is for you to bottle out.

Cus Damatio once said that the feeling of fear is as natural as the feeling of hunger and thirst or of wanting to use the toilet. When you're hungry you eat. When you're thirsty you drink, and so it should be with the feeling of fear. You shouldn't panic under it, you should harness and then utilise it. So my goal became to control and master fear, rather than to erase it.

Now came the hard part, putting theory into practice. I needed exposure to stressful situations in a bid to conjure up fear in the hope that in confronting that fear I would become desensitised to it, 'confrontation, desensitisation', if you like. How to go about it though? I couldn't just go out and look for trouble - that would be going against the strict moral and ethical codes of Karate, and also the law of Karma, 'A good for a good, and a bad for a bad'.
The only way I could find around this was 'bouncing' in the Coventry pubs and night-spots. But I had to ask myself if I could hack it: Coventry seemed more famous those days for the monopoly it held on violence than for its three spires and cathedral. I was riddled with self doubt. What if I got hammered? What if my bottle went? In the end the thought of living with my fears seemed to me to be worse than the fear of getting beaten up, in that the former was long term, and the latter short term. So began my term of office 'on the door'.

Please don't take this out of context, not everyone has a fear of fighting or a violently confrontational situation. What you fear may vary from spiders to a first speech, the concepts of overcoming those fears, however diverse they may appear, are the same, as I shall go into a little later.

CHAPTER FOUR

WHAT ARE YOU AFRAID OF?

This question should not be taken too literally, though the literal answer should already have been sought. It is one thing to admit your fears and quite another to analyse why we are afraid of those fears.

Your fear of making a big business decision may be due to a fear of failure, if the decision is a wrong one you may lose money, even your business. Your fear may be of success. If you make the right decision and your business doubles its turnover could you cope with the extra workload that would generate, taking in more stock taking on more staff, generally taking more risks?

Similarly, a judo practitioner is scared of taking his black belt. Why? Again he may fear failure. If he fails the grade he may be embarrassed, he may feel that he loses the respect of his colleagues. The failure of one grading, especially the prestigious black belt, may force him to give up hope and stop training.

He may also fear success. If he passes he will be looked up to by those of a lower grade, this will give him added pressure that perhaps he feels he can't cope with. He may fear getting injured or ridiculed. As a black belt he may have to take on extra responsibilities at the club where he trains, they may even ask him to teach. As a brown belt he feels comfortable but as a black belt he may feel pressured.

I remember well, as a child, first learning to swim and the first time that the teacher put me in the big group at the deep end of the pool. Now, in the shallow end I could swim up and down all day long. I felt safe in the shallow end because if things ever got a little too much for me, if I felt tired and wanted a rest, I knew that at any time I could place my feet on the floor.

When the teacher put me in the deep end I became frightened because, whilst I knew I could swim, I was worried that if anything went wrong or I wanted a rest I couldn't. The water was too deep for me to touch the floor. Subsequently, I couldn't swim in the deep end.

Many people feel this about confronting their fears. They feel that if they fail they may be ridiculed in front of their peers, and they wouldn't be able to handle it. If they succeed they feel that they will be out of their depth, and they wouldn't be able to handle that either.

I always feel that there is no such thing as failure, the fact that you have tried already makes you a success. The fact that you have tried also puts you well and truly on the first rung of the ladder to success. Of course there will be many people on the sidelines ready to see you fall, that's life, but ask yourself this. Who are these people? They are mere spectators in life whilst you are a player. You are not a failure because you do not make it you are a success because you tried.

Try to analyse why it is you have a fear of something and then come to terms with it. The three golden words to help you cope with the consequences of your actions, whether they are successful or not are, *I'll handle it.*

If I'm a success and I get added pressure, I'll handle it.

If things don't work out, I'll handle it.

If I fail my back belt, I'll handle it.

If I pass and get added pressure, Ill handle it.

If I lose my job, I'll handle it.

If I change jobs and don't like the new job, I'll handle it.

If my wife/husband leaves me, I'll handle it.

Worst case scenario
Look at the worst case scenario and tell yourself that if it happens *I'll handle it.*

No matter what it is that you fear, at the end of it will be *I won't be able to handle it.*

If I go to the dentist and he doesn't use enough pain killer, it'll hurt and I won't be able to handle it.

If I take that new job I might not be up to it and be ridiculed, I couldn't handle that.

If I give up my job and home to work/travel abroad and it doesn't work out, I couldn't handle it.

If I buy myself that new car and then lose my job I wouldn't be able to pay for it. I couldn't handle that.

A good example of this is an incident that happened to me after a particularly nasty incident in *Watch My Back*. After a battle with some soldiers myself and the doormen were herded into the manager's office, by the police, to watch the incident as recorded on the clubs c.c.t.v.. I quote:

Three policemen, two managers and four doormen squeezed into the tiny manager's office that had been tidied up especially. I tried to keep an 'I'm innocent officer' look on my face, but it wasn't easy knowing what was on film. Cigarette smoke herded the room and daggered my eyes. My brain buzzed and busied itself trying to analyse and assess the situation ahead of me. No one was speaking, all eyes hit the T.V. screen as it crackled in to life. Dave, the ultra thin, bespectacled manager, who was continually pushing the specs back up his nose, wound the tape forward to where it all began. I prayed that a miracle had occurred and I was off camera, or that the tape would suddenly, mysteriously break down. Dream on, I knew that I was going to be tonight's celluloid star. 'Play' was pressed and the silent movie began its recall. I hoped it was gong to be kind to me.

Initially it was. It showed us diligently trying to stop the quarrelling and then being attacked from behind by the unscrupulous, unprovoked soldiers as they left the club.

'Stop!' demanded the hefty Sergeant, whose clean cut, smart features put you more in mind of a bank manager than a policeman. My heart missed a beat. Dave dutifully put the tape on pause at the Sergeant's bidding. The Sergeant then pointed ominously to the screen.

'Who's that?'

His finger aimed at the dozen on screen, frozen in a second of muted, vehement viciousness, but more accurately at myself. The panic I felt inside was like I have never felt before. It engrossed my body like a rapidly enlarging growth that was forcing all the self control in my whole being outwards. I breathed in deeply, controlling it, captaining it, but still it pushed outwards fighting against me, hacking at my weakness with the sword of self doubt. My inner opponent went to work, 'you'll get locked up - there will be comebacks - you'll go to prison for this, PRISON, PRISON, PRISON!!' The ship of my moral fibre was under the threat of mutiny from the minority 'yellow crew' (inner opponent) within

*me. I cracked the whip of self control and herded the craven in me
back to captivity.*

   'That's me.'

   *I answered the Sergeant's question, hiding my inner turmoil.
His eyes searched mine for the weakness that he wouldn't find. It
was under lock and key.*

   'You used a duster,' he challenged.

   'No, I never used anything,' I lied, meeting his challenge.

   He by-passed my denial.

   'That's out of order son,' he said condemningly.

   *The silence rang in my ears for a long, long second (time
distortion), broken by the 'whirl' of the video as the Sergeant pressed
play on the video and all eyes left me for the screen. The voice of ill
reason (my inner opponent again) started again in my head. 'You're
scared. You're finished. Admit it, they've got you, they've got you.
Give in, give in. You're weak, you're weak, you're not strong
enough.' - Each trying to hook on to a ledge of weakness, but I
ignored the voice and countered consciously 'I'm not scared. They
haven't got me. I'm not finished. I'll never give in. I can handle it.'
Then I challenged my own mind (my inner opponent), 'give it
your best shot, I can handle anything that you throw at me.' I
knew from experience that your own mind can be your worst enemy
and that as soon as you give in, even a little bit, to these thoughts,
they grew stronger and stronger, feeding on each little victory, making
you weaker and weaker. The key was to fight back and not listen
to the voice. That was the only way to stop it.*

In this case the worst case scenario was, I could go to prison, I
told myself that if that happened *I could handle it.*

People feel that by taking chances they are risking security.
Security is knowing in your mind that, if it comes to the worst,
you can handle it.

I invested my last few pounds on self publishing one of my earlier books. I was really worried that if it didn't work out I would lose my savings so before I committed the money to the book I told myself that if it didn't work and the book flopped, I could handle it.

Remember, ships are safe in the harbour, but that is not what ships were made for.

You need to take chances if you want to expand. I read an apt saying in Susan Jeffers' book *Feel the Fear, and do it anyway*,

If you always do what you've always done, you'll always get what you've always got.

Which is very true. Life is like a huge supermarket full of all the things we want, but it is no different to an ordinary supermarket where you have to pay for the goods. The only difference is, in the supermarket of life the currency is time, dedication, commitment and pain. All the things are in there for anyone who is willing to pay the price, if you're not you'll always be a window shopper.

I worked hard to become a qualified wrestling coach, one of my friends said 'I'd love to be a wrestling coach.' As though the achievement was an impossible one. 'You can be one,' I told him, emphatically, 'Just give me your Fridays for the next year, oh and some dedication and pain, and you can be a wrestling coach.' He really did want to be a wrestling coach, but not that much, like most people he wanted something for nothing. What he failed to understand is that the certificate would mean nothing on its own, it's the year of confrontation, pain and dedication that spores the real goal.

The *if only* game

Similarly many people talk about the fact that they would 'love to do this, be that, go there, achieve that'. They talk from a negative view point that none of it would be realistically possible, but it is. When I tell them this they invariably reel out a long list of *if onlys*. They play the *if only* game.

If only I wasn't so busy I could study for that doctorate.

If only I didn't have a mortgage and a family I'd take a chance on running my own business.

If only I wasn't so committed here I'd sell up and travel the world.

If only I had the energy I'd study a different art to make my own more complete.

If only . . . if only . . . if only . . .' If only people would stop making excuses they would do something with their lives other than watch them go by. No matter what the circumstances there will always be an *if only*, especially if you are looking for one. *If only* is often just another way of saying *I'm scared to do it.* Packing up your job, selling your house and then travelling the world is not easy and there are a myriad of *if onlys* that stop thousands of people from doing it every day. But there are some that it does not stop: I've had friends of mine do it. There are dozens of *if onlys* that stop people from studying part time to become a lawyer, for instance, but Richard, a friend of mine, managed to do it whilst working two other jobs.

I've lost count of the number of people I know who would love to travel to America to train with some of the world's greatest martial artists. The *if onlys* would never allow it, though it never stopped Rick Young from travelling over twice a year and becoming a world renowned martial artist. Rick works as a postman in the day and teaches martial arts by night, so his *if onlys* must have been tremendous.

John Fenton, now a multi-millionaire, was brought up as a normal working class boy, but he didn't allow the *if onlys* to stop him becoming what he is today.

Bob Spour always wanted to be a lovey (an actor) so he gave up everything, work, money, the lot, to go to full time drama school and became just that.

Mike Tyson, probably the most talked about boxer this century, was plagued as a young man from fears much greater than himself, he had a mountain of *if onlys*, he didn't let them stop him becoming what he is now. If you really want something then nothing will get in your way, if you are afraid for whatever reason the mind will manufacture a thousand feasible *if onlys* to stem your flow.

So make sure that you can deal with the *if onlys* right from the offset, accept the risks that are involved, there will always be risks, if there were no risks there would be no problem and everyone would be living and leading happy and successful existences. Whilst this may seem a little peripheral to the subject of fear, it is not, it is our fears that stop us from achieving our goals.

CHAPTER FIVE

COMFORT ZONES

Most people find their own little niche in life, a comfort zone within which they feel safe. Whilst inside the parameters of their comfort zones they can pretty much do as they please without too much discomfort, as soon as they venture outside of those walls the fear starts.

Your comfort zone may be your job, your relationship, your martial arts club, your lifestyle, or for someone phobic it may be the confounds of your house. Your comfort zone may be anything on ground level if you are terrified of heights, or escalators, or crowds, or confined spaces or travelling in the car etc, etc. The list can go on and on. As a young person my fear was life itself. I was afraid of change.

My marriage
Whilst my marriage was not happy it was safe. I did not love the person I was with but was too scared to be without a partner.

If I split from my wife (my ex-wife now) I feared I'd lose access to my children and have nowhere to live. My self esteem was low so I also felt that I may not get another girlfriend, I was worried that someone else would want my wife if I left, (even though I didn't want her myself), afraid that I might leave and then realise that I really did love her after all and then she wouldn't have me back. I was afraid that the whole issue would grow out of my control and make me depressed, and if it did I felt that I wouldn't be able to handle it.

My job

Quite frankly my job was abysmal, I hated every minute of the seven years I worked as a chemical plant operator, but hey, it was safe, and jobs like that aren't that easy to come by (the best move I ever made was the day that I left that job). This of course was underlined by all of my work mates and many of my family members who felt that they just had to tell me how lucky I was to have such a good job.

I was scared to leave the job because I felt that there was too much risk involved: *What if I didn't find another job?* I wouldn't be able to pay the mortgage, they might take the house off me. *What would become of the family, my poor kids without a home?* I'd be a failure and everyone would say 'I told you so.'

I even worried about changes within the work place: if someone new was taken on I would worry about whether or not I'd get along with them.

What if they were objectionable people and the work place became a hive of arguments? I couldn't handle that, arguing every day, that would make me depressed and I hate being depressed.

If I was asked to take on extra responsibility it would get me down because I feared that I might not be up to it; I might fail and be ridiculed.

What If I succeeded? The managers would be pleased with that success and probably give me more responsibility and then I'll be stuck with it forever.

I was afraid of failure and at the same time I was afraid of success, I was afraid of change and yet, paradoxically I was also afraid of no change, this being conducive with me being stuck in a bad job for the rest of my life.

The fish bowl syndrome
People are a little like a gold fish in that they will only grow as big as the bowl you place them in.

If you put a gold fish in a small bowl he will not grow, put him in a big bowl and he will grow to accommodate the bigger bowl, if you put him in a pond he will expand yet again.

The fish bowl is our metaphoric comfort zone, to grow we have to continually extend the parameters of the bowl. Whilst this may be uncomfortable initially, it is the only way. Of course with the bigger bowl comes greater responsibility but that is all part and parcel of expanding. If I farm one acre of land and decide to take on another acre I will get twice the crop. But twice the crop will mean twice the work and responsibility. That should go without saying.

Pay-offs for not confronting and expanding
Expanding the comfort zone will add excitement and potential to your life, not expanding means staying exactly where we are. The reason most people do not expand are the pay-offs. Once you realise and accept this you will be ready to move.

1) Comfort zone
The first pay-off for not confronting your fears and expanding is the comfort zone.

This is an empty threat that the mind will make to keep you from growing. *If you grow you'll lose your comfort zone.* You do not really lose the comfort zone because it is replaced by a new one, and when that is broken it will be replaced yet again and again and again each time that you expand the comfort zone. Nothing is really lost though an awful lot is gained.

2) No rejection

One of the major fears of expansion is rejection. Many people have an innate fear of being rejected, by potential employers, partners, work mates, peers or simply a fear of being rejected by life. You may fear that your old friends will reject you because you become a success, your new associates reject you for daring to succeed.

If your family does not grow with you you may feel that they will reject you for growing alone, etc. Rejection is always a possibility, when I left my job as a night club doorman and made a success of writing I was surprised to find that many of my old friends began to reject me, perhaps they were jealous/ envious of my success, perhaps they thought me pretentious for daring to try, maybe they felt betrayed that I had expanded when and where they dare not. Whatever the reason the rejection was tangible and at first I found it very disconcerting, even discouraging. I also felt rejection as I tried to expand into new areas, many of my peers incredulous that I dared try to better myself and enter their world (I shall enlarge on this in a later chapter). This also bothered me, until I realised that rejection was their problem and not mine and would only effect me if I let it.

My friends of old who rejected me were obviously not really friends, the acid test of my success had proved that. Those in front of me, who I looked on as peers, were not worthy of the term, and if my success bothered them they were obviously insecure people who were on the way down and not up.

Rejection is a sign of other people's weaknesses and should not even be considered, only by-passed.

3) No failure
Another negative pay-off is *if I don't try I can't fail*. The act of not trying is a failure on its own, so if you do not try you have failed even to get to the starting line. However, if you do try it means you have succeeded already.

The real battle is not with the elements it is with yourself.

If you are frightened to enter a race in case you lose but enter the race anyway, whether you win the race or not is irrelevant because you have beaten yourself by entering against your own will.

Entering a marathon is a good example, the majority of people do not enter a marathon to win they are entering to complete the course, if and when they do they are elated simply because they have finished the course. Some see success as the fact that they have beaten their own previous record.

A woman who had a fear of eating in busy restaurants finally decided to challenge her fear and, for the first time, arranged to visit a particularly busy restaurant that night with her husband. She managed to get right to the restaurant doors but, on hearing the busy hum of voices inside she could go no further and had to leave.

All the way home in the car she cried because she felt that she had failed. Until her husband pointed out that, reaching the restaurant doors was a great success because on previous attempts she had not even got to the stage of booking a table. Using this as a catalyst she was eventually able completely to confront her fears of busy restaurants once and for all.

A young child who walks for the first time is not a failure because he only takes two steps, he is a success because he has never walked before, he is not a failure when he walks only five steps he is a success because, whilst five steps may not seem a lot, it is still two steps better that three.

Failure is a negative word that really does not exist. I would probably learn more from a failure than a success, so in reality failure is just an alternative set of experiences. We learn from success how to succeed, we learn from failure how not to fail and subsequently how to succeed. I have been down a few avenues that didn't work for me but the experience was invaluable, things were learned that could never have been learned in any other way. As Billy Connolly said, 'That's why there is a rubber at the end of your pencil!'

As they say, *The man who has not made a mistake has not done anything*.

4) You hate where you are, but at least you can handle it
I might not be very happy with my lot, but at least I can handle it. Many people feel that they can handle what they have now but taking on any more would be too much. You have to believe that you can handle more and tell yourself that you can or, again growth will not be imminent. We are not talking about confronting all your fears at once and going from a fish bowl straight into a huge pond, that would be unrealistic and could cause disorientation. Rather we are talking about very gradual steps that will slowly but surely expand your comfort zone.

When I first started weight training I could bench press 60lb, with a struggle, whilst my training partner could push an impressive 160lb. To me this seemed an impossible feat. If I had have tried there and then to lift 160lb it would indeed have been impossible, however, by pyramiding the weight, slowly increasing the amount I lifted over the next six months, expanding the physical comfort zone of how much I could lift by a few pounds at a time, I too was able to push 160lb and later as much as 250lb. Something that I would never have thought possible I now handled with ease.

My original physical comfort zone of 60lb became so light that it was not even heavy enough for me to use as a warm up weight.

Similarly a shop floor worker in the factory does not expect to go straight to company chairman. He may go in very steady steps from labourer to machinist, then to shop floor foreman, later to senior foreman then management and later to company chairman.

So expand the comfort zone, find your feet and become orientated with the new altitude and then expand again and if the doubts about your ability to handle it come flooding in tell yourself that you can and will handle it. Risk is the cavernous hole that lies between those that dream and those that do. If there was no risk there would be no point, everyone would have everything they wanted.

5) Security
Security is another pay-off for staying and not expanding, a little like myself when I worked at the chemical plant, I hated the job but the thought of losing my security by moving to a new and better job, by expanding my comfort zone, kept me glued to the spot, especially when this was underlined by those around me. Security is no more than being able to handle anything that life throws at you and if you expand your comfort zone at a gradual pace then your security need never be compromised anyway. Many people spend their whole lives

planning and saving for the rainy day syndrome that never comes, never really taking chances and never really enjoying what they have. Some end up dying with a lot of money in the bank having lived a relatively empty life. I have a friend whose father is a little shy when it comes to spending any of his 'hard earned money'. Even though he has plenty of it, he lacks many of the luxuries of life that he would like because he daren't spend. He fears that spending will compromise his security.

When his son told him that he should enjoy his money he replied 'when I die, you'll inherit all my money.' His son said, 'I don't want your money when you're dead, I want you to enjoy it now, when you're alive.' This obviously hit home because he went out the next day and brought his wife a new kitchen.

The Chinese say, *If you earn two pennies spend one on food to live and one on flowers to give you a reason to live.*

This is what I call *The When Complex*.

When I've got a safe amount of money in the bank I'll . . .

> *have the car that I've always wanted.*
>
> *take my dream holiday.*
>
> *buy my lady a new kitchen.*
>
> *do a little less overtime.*
>
> *buy the Rolex watch that I've always said I'd buy when the money was there.*

It's a copout. Similar to saying when I feel better about myself I'll confront my fears/finish the relationship/start the new relationship . . .

When I'm a little fitter I'll join the gym.

When I'm a little more financially secure I'll start my own business.

When I'm more confident I'll join the Karate/Judo/boxing club.

When, of course, often never comes, or if it does it is extended with another *when*.

People do not live for fear of risking their security so they end up becoming secure but unhappy and unfulfilled. Paradoxically many become very insecure in their secure units because they live in fear of external disruption like losing their jobs and the likes.

When you have come to terms with and can accept that there is far more to gain than there is to lose, expansion and confrontation becomes a more viable concept.

CHAPTER SIX

STEP TWO

A lot of people do nothing about their fears simply because they do not know how. Even once they have analysed all we have covered in the previous chapters they still don't know how to go about conquering their fears.

In this chapter I should like to offer the reader a road map, if you like, to help on the journey from pain to personal power. I know that, possibly, some of you out there will be getting a little impatient and wanting me to cut to the chase. That would be very easy to do, it would also save me a lot of time, but, unfortunately it would not help you the reader. Like painting the woodwork in your house, priming and preparation are pivotal if a good and lasting job is to be achieved. If you prepare the surface and apply a good undercoat the glossing is so much easier and the finish so much more professional, if you don't prepare you only do half a job.

These are a few of the things that people do not understand that need to be understood.

1) Planning to venture into the threatening situation.

It is important that the reader has a game plan and definite, though achievable, goals. It's very easy to lose direction and energy if you haven't got a 'road map' from where you are to where you want to go. When I travel from one city to another teaching I always acquire 'directions', if I didn't I probably wouldn't get there, and if I did it would definitely take me a lot longer and subsequently I'd use up a lot more fuel.

In this case the road map will be from *how you feel and where you are now* to, *how you want to feel and where you want to be at the end of the journey*. This can be achieved using the *fear pyramid* (detailed later).

My own game plan was to go from a position of personal weakness to a position of power by systematically confronting my fears, one by one, starting with my least fears and gradually building up through and to my bigger fears. I realistically saw myself, on my road map, as a weak person who was afraid of many things, especially my bodily reactions to confrontation and change. A person not in charge of his own life and therefore his own destiny.

My destination was personal power, at the end of my metaphoric journey I wanted to be in charge of me. I knew that real power was not in being able to get others to do what I wanted rather to be able to get myself to do what I wanted. My goal therefore was to be able to live a brave and exciting life where I was not under the dominion of every little fear that happened to pass by. My strategy was to do this by confronting and gaining exposure to my fears. What you might call paradoxical intention. After all, what we resist persists. My intention was not to try and find a route around fear, there isn't one, rather to go the direct route right through the heart of it.

So you need to know where you are now and where you want to be. A tangible goal will give you definite direction.

2) Coping with the anticipation of failure.
From my experience anticipation is usually far worse than confrontation. It is reported that 95% of all the things we fear never happen, therefore 95% of the time we are worrying for nothing. The way to deal with this is to take a close look at

what failure is, and whatever it is, accept it. Tell yourself that *you can handle it*. As I said before risk is the cavernous hole between those that dream and those that do. It is risk that separates the *talkers* from the *walkers*, it sorts out the men from the boys. Risk is the barrier that places 95% of the success with 5% of the populace, that 5% being those that accept risk as part and parcel of confrontation.

Whenever I am confronted by a particularly pressing situation, whether it is taking a risk with an investment or dealing with someone who wants to meet me on the common for a fight I look at *worst case scenario*. If I make this decision/take on this challenge/confront my fear/leave my wife/job etc, what is the worse thing that could happen? Whatever it is I tell myself that *I can handle that*.

If I lose money or even my business taking a chance on an investment, I'll handle it.

If I meet that monster on the common and I get a good hiding, I can handle that.

I remember once having to appear on a popular T.V. programme to do a national phone-in on self protection with me as the expert answering the viewers' questions and offering advice. Now, I've appeared frequently on the T.V. and I usually cope very well with it, however, on this occasion I was expected to appear for some 15 minutes live. In 15 minutes it would be very easy to trip up and make myself look an absolute fool. It was made worse by the fact that everyone around me felt it was their job to tell how silly I would look if I did trip.

Initially it all got to me and I started listening to these, probably well intentioned mates (mates??). Eventually I came to my senses and had a good think about the show. I made plans to study my subject well before the show, and, if everything went wrong and I looked silly in front of the whole nation, I'd handle it. If looking silly was the worse thing that could happen, I could handle that standing on my head. I also told my friends and associates not to talk to me if all they had to offer was negativeness. I told them that if I did look daft at least I was out there having a go, I had already succeeded where they had failed by actually appearing on the show. Once I had accepted that I could handle *worst case scenario* my fears disappeared and the show was a success (even if I say so myself).

So, look at the worst thing that could happen and tell yourself, *I can handle it*. Also remember that there is no such thing as failure, only different experiences, all of which offer a lesson.

3) Enlisting the help of those who are sympathetic.
Don't hesitate to enlist the help of others, especially those who understand your dilemma. I have many students who ring me on a regular basis for help, support and an occasional dose of inspiration. A problem shared is a problem halved. If you have no one close to you who can help join a support group or seek inspiration or answers from books and tapes. I always used to read books that inspired me to succeed, later to inspirational talk tapes or music. Inspiration is a particularly important aspect that needs topping up daily. Every time you feel a little down or if you feel as though you can't go on, listen to a tape or read a book to kick-start your flagging ego.

4) Dealing with the unpredictable behaviour of others.

As a paradox to this avoid negative people who, for whatever reason, do not want you to succeed. People can often be very fickle, even those whom you think are your friends can suddenly become messengers of foreboding. I always made a point of avoiding these people or simply taking them to one side and asking them why they insist on putting me off. There is no need to fall out with these people, just ask them, 'why are you being so negative?' or, 'if you can't offer me encouragement I'd rather you kept your thoughts to yourself'. More than anything do not take in any of the negativeness, you have to learn to close your ears to these types of people. I remember a friend of mine actually scoffing when I told him that I was going to try and become a full time writer, he more or less told me not to get above my station. And my ex-wife (note she is now ex) telling me to 'grow up' and 'people like us (working class people) don't write books.'

These were just two of several that I had from some of my so called friends, and I don't mind telling you that the comments cut me to the quick. Those who refused to grow with me are still where they were when I left them, sometimes if people will not grow with you you have to leave them behind (more on this subject later).

5) Finding alternatives to running away from fear.

There is more than one way to skin a cat, as the old saying goes. If a direct assault on your fear is too much to contemplate break the fear down in to smaller components that are a little more manageable or try perhaps to come in at a different angle. Breaking the fear down in to smaller components (to be detailed later) can mean confronting manageable fragments of the fear until the whole unit is confronted and overcome. One of my early fears was of spiders, rather than just jumping in the deep end (which can work well for some) and picking up a spider I spent a little time studying the spider from a distance, gradually getting closer and closer, then touching the spider with an extension, a piece of stick or a pencil, so that I could get used to the sudden movements of the spider and later still touching the spider with my finger. Eventually I was able to pick up the spider and let in crawl over my hand without any fear or discomfort. Coming in from a different angle may mean, as a for instance, building confidence by talking to someone who has already trod the same path and overcome the fear, or even watch someone else do what you are afraid to do.

When I went to buy my first new car I had a terrible fear that by getting the car through my business and on finance I would be getting out of my depth. I worried that I could not really afford the car, even though I knew that I could, I worried that my business might fail and I would not be able to afford the repayments. For some perverse reason I also felt that I was, in some way, not worthy of such an expensive car. Rather than directly confront my fear by going out and purchasing the vehicle I phoned up a business associate, someone who was familiar with my business and who had, over the years, had several expensive company cars, and asked his opinion.

I started the conversation negatively by telling him that I wasn't going to get the car because I couldn't afford it. Without any hesitation he told me that I should go right out and get the car, 'You and I both know that you can afford it, and if you don't get it now you'll always regret it'. He said it emphatically. Of course I knew that he was right and that I was worrying for nothing. Speaking to him gave me the confidence to go out and get the car and I never did regret it, nor was there ever a time when I could not afford the payments. Having said that, if the business couldn't stand the payments I would have perhaps been unwise to make the purchase.

Sun Tzu said that before you wage war first count the costs. Count the costs and make sure that you are ready to handle the outcome, whatever it may be.

Draw up your road map and check out the worst case scenarios at the beginning of the journey and always tell yourself that no matter what happens you'll handle it.

CHAPTER SEVEN

THE INNER OPPONENT

The ugly hand maiden of fear is the omniscient Mr Negative, General Sun Tzu called him the inner opponent, Susan Jeffers called him the chatterbox, I call him Mr Negative.

The inner opponent is the negative voice that perches on the shoulder of your mind's eye and tells you that you're frightened, scared or that you 'can't handle it' (the situation). Many people are not beaten by their fear, rather they are beaten by their own minds. A negative notion that latches onto a subconscious insecurity soon grows in to a monstrously big 'inner opponent' that forces people to acquiesce a lot sooner that they should. The inner opponent is responsible for beating more people that any tangible or intangible fear. It is fair to say that if you cannot beat the man on the inside then you cannot beat the man on the outside.

I remember a wonderful story about a wrestler who was travelling by train from Glasgow to London to wrestle the legendary Bert Asarati, renowned for 'hurting' his opponents. All the way down on the train journey the wrestler fought with his inner opponent who kept on reminding him of the prowess of Mr Asarati. Every time the train stopped at a station the wrestler's inner opponent tempted him to get off and go back to Glasgow, at each station the inner opponent getting stronger and stronger, the wrestler's will getting weaker and weaker. By Birmingham the wrestler could stand no more. He got off the train and took the next train back to Glasgow. Mr Asarati received a note from the wrestler that said, 'Gone back to Glasgow, you beat me in Birmingham'.

His inner opponent defeated him hours before he was due to enter the ring.

This story will be familiar to many, only the opponent may not have been an 18 stone wrestler, rather a big business deal, the decision to change job/home/car/relationship, ask the boss for a rise, travel the world, start up a new business, expand an existing business. To the phobic it may have been leaving the house, going in a plane, travelling in a car, going in a lift, up a travellator etc. Many are beaten before the fight by their own minds. Why? Because it takes no effort to think negative thoughts, the inner opponent will do that for you, to think positive thoughts however takes a lot of effort. This from James Clavel's book Shogan,

To think bad thoughts is really the easiest thing in the world. If you leave your mind to itself it will spiral you down into ever increasing unhappiness. To think good thoughts, however, requires effort. This is one of the things that training and discipline are about. So teach your mind to dwell on sweet perfumes, the touch of silk, tender rain drops against the shoji, the tranquillity of dawn, then at length you won't have to make such an effort and you will be of value to yourself.

Left to its own devices the mind can be a self-detonating time bomb of negativeness that will spiral you down into ever increasing misery. Dealing with the inner opponent is firstly about understanding that everyone has an inner opponent, though very few come to terms with him, and understanding that we will never reach our full potential whilst he has the run of our heads. Mr negative is very controllable, if you know how.

These are three ways that I have found successful in dealing with Mr Negative.

1) Thought rejection

Reject the negative thoughts by completely ignoring them, not listening to anything that Mr negative says, thus leaving him no mental ledge on which to perch.

This is harder than it seems and demands self discipline. Negative thoughts have a habit of swimming into your mind, uninvited and at will. Don't have any of it. It is your mind, you are in charge. Occupy your mind by reading, listening to the radio, by keeping yourself busy, watching the box, anything to take your mind away from the negative thoughts. Don't give in and panic with the thoughts because that will cause them to multiply tenfold and then twenty fold, before you know it your mind has been over run by negative emotion that can quickly turn to depression. So, just ignore them.

2) Thought counter attack

If you can't come to terms with this try thought counter attack (this is the method that I practice). Fight your inner opponent by countering every 'negative' thought he throws at you with a 'positive' thought of your own.

Inner opponent	*You're scared.*
Your counter	*No, I'm not scared.*
Inner opponent	*You can't handle this situation.*
Your counter	*Yes, I can handle this situation, I can handle anything.*
Inner opponent	*You're out of your depth, you'll never cope.*
Your counter	*I'm not out of my depth and I can cope, in fact I'll cope easily.*

Inner opponent   *You'll fail and everyone will laugh.*
Your counter   *If that's the worse that can happen, I*
                      can handle it.

3) Repetitive mantra
You can block out the negative conversations with repetitive mantras.

I can handle it . . . I can handle it . . . I can handle it . . . I can handle it . . . I can handle it.

I'm in charge . . . I'm in charge . . . I'm in charge . . . I'm in charge . . . I'm in charge.

I'm not scared . . . I'm not scared . . . I'm not scared . . . I'm not scared . . . I'm not scared. etc.

The list goes on and on. By countering your inner opponent you will erase the negative thoughts with the positive. You have to learn not to take any crap from the inner opponent and fight, tooth and nail, every time that he rears his ugly head. Watch out though, he can be a cheeky beggar, if you are not vigilant he will try to sneak in when you least expect. Even the feelings that accompany negativeness can be countered with defiance. I always tell myself, 'Do your worst, I can handle it, I can handle twice what you're giving me'. The biggest fight is always with yourself and the more wins you get under your belt the stronger you become and the weaker your inner opponent becomes. Once you have the inner opponent under control you are well on the way.

Fight back negativeness right from the onset. Each negative thought you allow to penetrate your psyche may and usually does erode a small part of your 'will' until eventually you are defeated. I work on the premise that *negative begets negative, begets defeat*. As a parallel, *positive begets positive, begets victory*. Your greatest enemy in times of adversity is your own mind. Tell your inner opponent that *you can handle it*.

Once you have come to terms with Mr Negative and have learned to accept fear as a friend, allow adrenalin the run of your body, don't allow yourself to panic. Knowledge is power. By understanding your own body, by understanding the mechanics of adrenalin/fear you can learn self control. Panic is catalysed by ignorance, by not understanding your own body, or its workings. Most people, in most situations are not defeated by their assailants, they are defeated by their own mind. Whilst the feeling of fear can be uncomfortable it cannot hurt you, it is a natural feeling that should be accepted without panic. There is no way around these feelings, everyone feels them, they are a part and parcel of adversity.

The feeling of fear (adrenalin) is as natural as the feelings of hunger and thirst or the feeling of wanting to use the toilet. When you feel hungry you don't panic, you eat, when you feel thirsty you drink. So it is with fear. Don't panic, act.
Cus Damatio.

CHAPTER EIGHT

THE TREATMENT

In brief and to be blunt the best way to overcome a fear is to confront it. This process is called *exposure therapy*. By exposing yourself to the fear you become desensitised to it. Learning only takes place whilst you are actually inside the confrontational situation the same as you can only practice swimming whilst immersed in the water.

The A, R & O Theory of fear control

My own theory of fear control, derived from many years of facing violence as a way of life in society's culture dish, the nightclub, consists of giving adrenalin the run of your body until you are ready to channel it. A little like drinking water that flows around a tank released with the turn of a tap. As a young person I was, unfortunately, at the mercy of my own adrenal gland, when the adrenalin flowed, I ran. I made the classic error of mistaking adrenalin for fear and thus, thinking myself a coward. I also felt that I was the only person in the world who felt this way.

A R & O? Accept, recognise and override. Accept fear into your body, recognise that it is adrenalin and then over-ride it by dealing with the adversity.

The cut out button

Generally the inner opponent does not allow us full control of our own mind, implanting thoughts that we would rather not be thinking, if it says, *Stop*, we generally do just that, if it says, *Don't fight it, you'll fail* generally we do not fight it (what ever it my be) and subsequently fail by not trying.

The brain has been installed with an automatic 'cut out' button, built-in by nature to protect the body and mind from 'burn out'.

Due to evolution (and a distinct lack of pre-historic animals in our everyday lives) and soft living this automatic 'cut out' is often set at a very low tolerance point, the slightest hint of stress or pain and the brain 'cuts out', leaving us well short of our desired goal because we capitulate far too readily. This is why it is said that most people go to their graves with their best songs still in them.

Extending cut-out

This 'cut out' button can and has to be extended if we want to attain any measure of success in our lives (everybody's 'cut out' point is set at a different tolerance, some people are gifted with a very high tolerance level). This is achieved simply by mastering the inner opponent and gradually stretching our own limits until we are at our full potential.

The pain barrier

Just past the 'cut out' point for those who push through it is the infamous 'pain barrier'. Extending/erasing the 'cut out' point is the pot of gold at the end of the metaphoric rainbow. This goal will not be acquired without an epic and arduous battle with your own mind. You must 'dare' yourself to take the challenge. Remember the old adage of the S.A.S., *Who dares Wins*.

Summary

In brief: when you feel fear, recognise it as a natural bodily reaction to confrontation, accept its presence calmly without panic, counter any negative thoughts and override them.

Adrenal exposure
Pain, fear, exhaustion, boredom and low esteem and the inner opponent will all, at one time or another (sometimes they may all strike together) gnaw away at your weaker links trying to make you quit, give in, surrender, capitulate. Over-coming and defeating these elements will greatly extend the 'cut out' point and help to develop a strong character, greatly heightening your self esteem.

The indomitable spirit
It is possible, eventually, to completely erase the 'cut out' point, where, in theory, you could find that nothing would be beyond achievement. This, though, is singularly the most difficult goal to achieve, known as the illusive *indomitable spirit*. The more that you experience and confront the 'fear' syndrome the more desensitised you will become to it and the easier it will be to control and thus harness. The more that you *confront and control* the stronger minded you will become. These exercises in *confront and control* will build the mental muscle as a bar bell and weights will build physical muscle, the same dictum *no pain, no gain* is also evident.

This gained strength of mind will put your whole life into perspective, all of a sudden those mundane tasks at work or around the home become a simple challenge by comparison, all are relegated to simple exercises in self-discipline, everything that life throws in your way become *challenges* that you will no longer balk at, nothing will seem beyond the purlieus of your mental capacity.

CHAPTER NINE

PRINCIPLES OF EXPOSURE THERAPY

1) Understand your fear and the subsequent reaction to it.
By understanding that fear is a natural fraction of any confrontational situation and that your bodily reactions to it, ie. adrenal reaction, are completely natural you will be better prepared.

When I learned that everyone felt fear and adrenalin was the friend of exceptional people, confronting my fears became a much easier task. Understanding that I hadn't failed because I still felt fear and that I and everyone feels fear when confronting new situations helped me immeasurably. I always thought the goal was to become fearless (it isn't) so I understandably felt like a failure every time I felt scared. When I later realised that fear was the natural bodily reaction felt by everyone and that the goal was to learn control, again this acted as a calming balm. It's very hard to get somewhere, no matter how hard you try, when you have the wrong map. It was also soothing to be told that by trying I had already been successful, it was only when you didn't try that you failed.

2) Enter the fear syndrome.
A scared young boxer named Cassius Clay (Mohammed Ali) fearfully approached his first entry to a boxing ring. A wise old boxing trainer, seeing that Clay was scared to enter the ring said to the young fighter, 'son you should always confront those things that you fear'.

Plan ahead, don't enter blind. Imagine the good the bad and the ugly. Mentally rehearse and visualise how you are going to react in all cases. See yourself 'handling' set backs positively, see yourself regaling in victory. Also imagine the consequences of success and the things, good and bad that it might bring. See yourself handling these also. I always pictured myself the victor and used this as inspiration, I also looked at the worst case scenario and visualised myself handling that gracefully.

I remember wanting to start training at a boxing club because I knew the exposure to good pugilists would help me with my own training in Karate. However I was worried that if I joined I might get knocked out. The pain element didn't worry me, it was more the embarrassment if it should happen. I knew that nothing of any worth ever came without risk so I visualised myself as an excellent boxer, this inspired me. I also watched a lot of boxing tapes and talked to boxers to gain yet more inspiration. Then I considered the worst case scenario and told myself that if I got knocked out, I could handle it. Two years later I became an A.B.A. boxing coach. I know many people who want the same qualification but cannot get over the cavernous *risk hole*.

As with my doing the boxing and using friends for support and inspiration, don't worry about enlisting the help of others, use them as a crutch. You may be surprised at the help you will get if only you ask. Eventually, as your confidence grows you can discard the crutch, something that needs to be done at some stage, and continue unaided. Again, avoid those who might feed you with negative instead of positive data. One of my friends told me I was 'mad' going to a boxing club, 'You'll end up with brain damage.' He said, then almost as an afterthought, 'but, if it's what you want to do . . .' Yea! Thanks for the encouragement. Others said, 'What do you want to do that for? Aren't you happy with what you've got?' As though my ambition was a greedy and selfish indulgence. Along the way you will quickly learn who to speak to and who to ignore.

One of my friends, Neil Adams, world champion and Olympic silver medal Judo player, reputedly the best judo player ever outside of Japan, is a great example of entering the fear syndrome to expand. Neil was winning just about everything there was to win in Judo and it was obvious to all that he had major potential. However he was rapidly becoming a huge fish in a small pool and was having to travel ever further afield to find competition. No one locally was testing him and he had far outrun his present teachers. It was getting to the stage where he was teaching them as opposed to them teaching him. At this point many would have sat back on their laurels and remained on the plateau that they had reached. They never really improve from that point on. Neil realised this and at a very young age, moved away from his parents to live in London, this enabling him to train full time at the Kodakan under the tuition of some of the world's finest Judoka.

He made many sacrifices to get there, not least having to become a small fish in a big pond, but he felt the risk was worth it to get where he wanted to be. From reading Neil's autobiography it is obvious that he had to go through a lot of adversity in this tough club, but in the end he shone through. If it wasn't for his decision to move to London and train with the best, it is very doubtful that he would have reached the level he did.

3) Don't be afraid of your bodily reactions to confrontation.
It has been said that we have nothing to fear in life but fear itself. This is a lot closer to the truth than people might imagine. Anticipation is certainly more uncomfortable than confrontation. People often become so wrapped up in their fears that, in the end, they become more scared of the feelings that accompany confrontation than they do of the object of their fear. As I formerly mentioned, when you over anticipate it opens the door for Mr negative who, spotting your weakness,

goes to work, engineering the weakness until it becomes a gaping hole that he can walk right through. Once he gets through in mass you are sure to lose, most likely before you even get to within distance of your confrontation. As with the wrestler coming from Glasgow to fight Bert Asarati in London, you too will lose the fight at Birmingham. This will only happen if you become afraid of the feelings that are associated with confrontation, so don't be afraid of them.

'Easy to say!' I hear you cry. Listen I've been there thousands of times and know the feeling well. That's all they are, feelings. They can't hurt you on their own. It is only your own panic that helps the feelings to burgeon. If you don't panic and tell yourself that you can handle it, they will eventually dissipate.

No one feeling can last for ever,
Remember this when you endeavour
To conquer fear and when depression creeps
In your mind this knowledge you should always keep.

This is a little poem that I used as a mantra whenever I was in a tricky situation and things started to feel ugly. No one feeling can last forever, it's true. Remember it and when things feel ugly for you, remind yourself, 'It can't last forever'. Also remind yourself that the feelings, however unnatural they may feel, ARE natural feelings that everyone, at some time, feels, and they will only take control if you let them, so don't. It's your mind, it's your body, you're in charge and nobody else.

The more you are able to stay in the exposed situation the more you will realise that all I've stated is true. The more you become desensitised to the feelings of adrenalin the stronger you will develop your mental muscle. No exposure no expansion. Lots of exposure lots of expansion. Be positive, control the inner opponent and there is nothing that you are not capable of.

4) Be active

I've always said, and we all know, that there are those that dream and there are those that do. I've been both in my time so can categorically say that dreaming as a single entity is about as useful as sugar wellingtons in a rain storm. If you do nothing but dream you will achieve nothing. It is those that act who make those dreams reality. Dreaming is very good if you marry it with action, it can act as a great stimulus and be very inspirational and inspiration is rocket fuel that will enable you to reach the stars. Dreaming is a form of visualisation, a great way of seeing where you want to go, who you want to be, what you want to do. But, as I keep reiterating, if you want to learn to swim you have to get wet. So keep active, whether large or small do something every day to get where you want to be and never put off until tomorrow, for dreamers tomorrow never comes.

Draw out your road map, set your sights on realistic goals and go for it.

Think of your journey like a 120 mile walk from Birmingham to London. If you try to do it all in one go you are setting yourself up for disappointment. Be realistic, set yourself an achievable distance to do every day. If you think that you are comfortable with eight miles a day stretch yourself and go for 10 miles a day. In twelve days you will have achieved your goal, where as if you had attempted the whole 120 miles in one or perhaps two goes you may well have taken on too much and gotten disheartened, eventually aborting the journey like so many people do.

I had a friend who wanted to get out of a bad relationship but was too afraid to leave. Just upping and going was something that he felt incapable of doing. He'd gotten to the stage where he was very miserable in his marriage but felt that there was no life for him outside of the marriage. His self esteem was very low.

Rather than jumping in the deep end and just leaving his wife he prepared himself very gradually by spending more and more time out of the marital home. It wasn't easy, his wife didn't like it and he had to fight every step of the way.

Whilst he was away from the house he took on a job that allowed him to socialise. He started to make many friends, this helped him to rebuild his broken confidence. He had also been afraid that if he left he might be homeless, having checked up on the 'house for rent' market he realised how simple getting a place of his own could be, some of his new friends had also offered him a room should he ever need it. Right towards the end of his marriage he even started going on overnight trips with some of his friends. Very soon he was spending more time out of the marital home than he was in it. When he eventually found the courage to leave it was not such a shock, after all, he'd spent the past 6 months preparing and practising. He also came to realise that most of the things that he was afraid might happen were very unlikely to, and if they did, he told himself, he would handle it.

5) Practice makes perfect.
Although I might be stating the obvious here, practice is the only way of growing. If you practice you will get stronger, if you don't you won't.

No one ever got rich by just looking at the stock market, no one ever got a beach physique by just staring at the weights, no one ever got successful by just lying in bed and dreaming about being successful, no one ever became a world class martial artist without getting out there and practising.

Whilst it is true that the more you practice the quicker you will improve it is also true that if you don't practice regularly enough your improvement will be very slow and there is more chance of you aborting the journey. So try to do something every day. If you leave it too long between training sessions it is likely that the body will forget what it has learned and you end up back at square one again. Use the inspiration of even the smallest success to fuel your next step by getting back to it as soon as possible, if you leave it too long between practice sessions the inspirational fuel may be lost. This is especially so with phobics. Even one step forward is better than staying stationary or moving backwards and every single step counts. Taken on its own one step may seem insignificant, added to all the other steps taken over the period of one year, it is quite a distance. So practice, practice, practice and don't worry that it is hard, if it was easy everyone would be fearless and hugely successful.

6) Be realistic and fair to yourself.
Being realistic is knowing your own limitations, try not to bite off more than you can chew. If you do take on too much and suffer a set back be fair to yourself, so many of my friends beat themselves up over silly setbacks. The fact that you are out there trying means that you are already a success. There will be many stumbles on the road to a powerful self, even falls, so you have to prepare for them. Success is not in never falling it is in always rising after falling. You must learn to be knocked down seven times and get up eight. I don't know anyone who

did not, at one time or another stumble or fall. A stumble or fall is just another learning experience and the lessons learned cannot be learned in any other way. Recovering from a stumble or a fall and learning never to give in develops real character. True character is never really tested until you hit the deck. Like the boxers, it is not just about how big a punch you can throw it's about how big a punch you can take. Whilst we endeavour not to stumble or fall we also prepare ourselves for its eventuality, just in case. How do we prepare? By telling ourselves over and again that, whatever happens, I can handle it.

If it does happen, pick yourself up, tend to your wounds and start again. Don't add insult to injury by letting your inner opponent tell you how bad it was of you to fall, how silly you looked when you fell, how ashamed you should be for falling, how you'll never recover from the fall, how everyone must be laughing at you falling and *hey, I told you you couldn't do it, I knew you'd fall. Who the hell do you think you are for even trying?*

If you allow the inner opponent a podium he will make you feel ashamed for trying when really you should feel proud, he will make you feel pretentious when you should feel confident and ambitious, he will make you feel weak when you should feel strong. In brief the inner opponent will make you feel completely worthless and will use any stumble or fall to underline and substantiate his negativeness.

A pat on the back.
It is also easy to become negative about those times when you do succeed. It is very important to remind yourself of how well you are doing. I would often feel very disillusioned if I was not gaining as quickly as I would have liked, my inner opponent telling me what a failure I was. I remember when climbing my pyramid of fears and struggling to get past a particular

step. I was starting to feel strong and confident because I had managed to defeat fears on the lower steps of the pyramid, things that had hung over me for years, but, as soon as I stumbled on a particularly difficult fear my inner opponent was straight in there,

So, you thought you were strong. Not so strong now, are you? You're not strong at all, you're weak.

Straight away I reminded myself that I was not weak, hadn't I already overcome some of my long standing fears at the bottom of the pyramid? My inner opponent was quick to maliciously point out that anyone could have overcome them. They were just kids' stuff. *Get to something half hard and what do you do? You fold like a piece of paper. That's all you are, a paper weight.*

Again, and at the risk of over emphasising the point, if you are out there trying then you are already a success and are already strong, any step forward is just that, a step forward. It should not be undermined, and should always be congratulated. All past victories should be used to emphasise and underline the fact that you are getting stronger, whenever you struggle with a new challenge use your past victories to reap strength. I remember many times when facing adversity, dragging up past victories to gain inspiration and to use as a yard stick. When I had a particularly nasty gang after me I drew strength from the fact that it wasn't the first time I'd had people after me and 'hey, if I handled it last time then I could handle it just as well this time.'

Success is not how you feel but how far you have gone
Very often people judge success by how they feel as opposed to how far they have gone. This is not the right way to look at it because as we approach a new situation and as we expand to take on a new challenge we will feel fear. More than once I

remember thinking 'I can't be getting any better, I still feel scared', totally forgetting the early lesson that *fear will never go away as long as I continue to grow*, and *everyone feels fear when confronting new situations*. I had to remind myself not only of these lessons but also of the fact that many of the things that I had feared all my life I had left decimated in my wake and that I was now doing and achieving things that I never dreamed possible, even though I was not yet at the top of my fear pyramid I was already living a brave and exciting life and for the first time since I was a child I no longer felt at the mercy of my inner opponent.

It's a little like going on a hundred mile journey in your car. If the car breaks down after eighty miles it doesn't mean that the journey is over and it doesn't mean that once you have fixed the car you have to start again. No matter what happens you have still successfully travelled eighty miles and you still only have twenty miles to go. O.K. Your success has been slowed a little, but you can handle that. Take a positive attitude to your hurdles and pitfalls. If my car breaks down because I never put enough water in the engine before setting out then I'll learn from that, next time I set of on a long journey I'll make sure I top up the water first. Remember, it's not how you feel it's how far you have gone.

7) Use a helper

Don't be afraid of using a helper, preferably someone who has trod the same path and come through. Read books and listen to inspirational tapes. Inspiration is the fuel that will get you where you want to be, but it will need topping up regularly. When you feel inspired, act.

There is no better person to talk to than someone who is where you want to be, he will make you feel like you can walk on water. Even being around successful people will make you feel good, make you feel like you can achieve, confront, change, grow, succeed. If your will is a little low and no one is to hand, use the phone, write a letter, watch a video, listen to a tape. Just the fact that you are doing these things is an excellent sign because it means you are taking action and you are fighting and beating the inner opponent. No matter how bad you feel, just do it. I guarantee you'll feel better afterwards. Every time that you beat the inner opponent you will be developing a little more mental muscle. Making decisions and taking action means that you are taking control and control of the self is what makes success.

You don't have to do everything alone, even now I'll phone people if I need a little inspiration, or I'll read a book or listen to a tape. A good friend will allow you to let off steam when things aren't going quite to plan and he'll let you talk about plans and reap inspiration when they are. If your batteries are a little low use a crutch to kick start you back into action. Also, a helper who has trod the same path will invariably have had to overcome the same hurdles. So when you say, 'You'll never guess what happened to me today', he'll invariably say, 'Oh yea, I remember when that happened to me. This is what I did to get past it'. Knowing that someone else has gone through the same problems and overcome them will bring great solace. There is nothing worse than thinking that you are the only person in the world who is feeling/experiencing what you're feeling/experiencing. I remember ringing up my helper for advice on a particularly trying problem, feeling all the worse because I thought the problem unique to me, 'Oh, you don't want to worry about that,' he told me convincingly, 'exactly the same thing happened to me, it happens to nearly everyone'. I can't tell you the relief that I felt knowing that it wasn't just me and that the problem I was facing was a 'common' problem.

Where I used people as helpers then, I act as helper to others now, as will you. And when they speak to you fearfully about the things they are experiencing you will laugh to yourself and find it hard to believe that you too once felt the same way. In hindsight your old fears will seem silly as your new life will feel exciting.

Whilst it is not a nice thing you should also take strength from those around you who fall. I'm not saying that you shouldn't help those that might be struggling, of course you should, but there will be those you cannot help for whatever reason. Use their failure to give you strength. On one or two occasions on the door when my fellow doormen lost their bottle in the midst of a bad situation and left their post I would unashamedly reap strength from their lack. This is not a selfish thing, far from it, panic and submission has a habit of being infectious. If people around you are losing it, it is very easy for their weakness to drag you down also, so you have to go straight to the offensive and think, 'they're losing it and I'm still here, that means I'm strong. I'm not going to fall like them. I'm going to stick with it.'

You'll be surprised at how you can make this work for you. I've watched people who I'd previously thought were very strong, falling by the wayside whilst I continued on. I remember thinking 'I thought they were really strong people and look at me, I'm stronger than them. And I'm going to get even stronger'. So, good or bad, use it.

8) Group support.
This is not something that I have used personally but I still think that it is an excellent idea to surround yourself with people of the same ilk as yourself. You will be able to reap advice and enthusiasm from those above you and offer help to

those below. The learning experience from group therapy would be tremendous and the benefits unparalleled. Everything needed to help you overcome your fears will be in the one room. An inspirational experience.

9) Admit your fears to others.

Whilst this isn't imperative it may be helpful. It is hard to enlist the help of others if they don't know how you're feeling. In the early days my greatest helper was my mother. Of course as a young person I felt ashamed to admit to her how I was feeling in case she thought me weak, but, as she always told me, 'I can't help you if I don't know what it is you're worried about'. Some of the things that I was scared of made me feel ashamed, I was convinced that if I told anyone I would be a laughing stock and that my mum would rush me straight down the doctors. It turned out, to my absolute amazement, that my fears were quite natural and manageable. If I didn't admit those early fears to my mum I'd probably still be dealing with them to this day.

One of my friends was having terrible fights with his wife, she couldn't understand why he wouldn't take the wonderful new job that he'd been offered, a job that he'd been working towards for a long time, a job that promised them the lifestyle they had always dreamed of.

He wanted the job, but was afraid to take it in case it didn't work out, in case he couldn't handle the pressure of change. The job he had wasn't good but it was safe. He worried that if he didn't like the new job he might be tied to it by the subsequent lifestyle that came with it and by the higher mortgage payments that came with the new home that the higher salary would enable them to buy. His worst fear was that if everything went wrong he might lose his wife, and they were already arguing (his inner opponent constantly reminded him of this fact). In his frightened state he even wondered whether the arguing and rows was an omen that the job change was not right. He daren't tell his wife of his fears because she had always seen him as a strong man and he didn't want her to think otherwise. So, rather than tell her out right of his fears he made up covering excuses as to why he didn't want to take on the new job, excuses that his wife could not come to terms with.

When things finally came to a head and he did tell her of his fears he was astounded at her sympathetic and supportive response. What she made him realise what that he was not alone, whatever the outcome was, good or bad they would share it and they would always be together. With the help of his wife my friend took on the new job and with it a new and better lifestyle. The fact that he had confided in his wife also brought them closer together. If he hadn't have shared it, who knows?

10) Finish what you have started.
It is important once you have started to climb the fear pyramid to finish. It is very easy to attain a measure of success and then stop growing. If you want complete control you need a complete victory, if you only climb half or three quarters up the pyramid then you are only partially in control. The problem with partial control is it often lapses back to no control. A little like only taking half a course of antibiotics, you feel a lot better so you don't finish the prescribed course. The next thing you know you're ill again because the infection wasn't completely cured. Similarly when treating a cancer it is imperative that the whole tumour is removed or the patient will certainly regress as the tumour inevitably grows back to full strength. Often people

get close to the top of the pyramid and then stop, saying, 'well, I feel a lot better now, I'm happy with the fact that I've got this far. I don't need to confront that last fear, I think I've done enough already'.

Usually this is just an excuse that the inner opponent invents, one of many, to stop growth. So if you want complete control complete the course.

CHAPTER TEN

THE FEAR PYRAMID

I believe that anyone can conquer fear by doing the things he fears to do, provided he keeps doing them until he gets a record of successful experiences behind him.
Eleanor Roosevelt

The method that I employed, to generate and ultimately control fear was the fear pyramid. This can often be a very private thing. A lot of people will not wish to share their more private fears with others, this reticence is understandable, though as stated earlier it is hard to enlist the help of others if you do not tell them what it is you fear. It is imperative, though, that you do admit them, even if it is only to yourself, don't fob yourself off as I once did with feeble excuses like, 'I'm not scared of it (whatever 'it' may be), I just don't want to do it', and other such inanities.

That is the first and most important step, you can go no further until this is complete. These are the three preparatory steps.

1) Make a List of all your fears.

2) Draw yourself a pyramid with as many, or as few, steps up to the pinnacle as you have fears.

3) Fill each of those steps with one of your listed fears starting at the bottom of the pyramid with your least fear and finishing at the top step with your greatest fear. (See illustration).

The common factor with all fears is that confronting them will cause an adrenal rush, it is anticipation that sparks adrenalin, as opposed to the actual fear itself.

FRED'S FEAR PYRAMID

VIOLENT
CONFRONTATIONS

SPARRING

KARATE
COMPETITIONS

DENTIST

SPIDERS

This is a hypothetical example, I've no doubt that your pyramid will be filled with completely different fears to Fred's.

Fred has filled his pyramid with all his own fears. He is scared of spiders, but of all his fears this one is his least, because of this, and the fact that we do not want to try and run before we can walk, we will get Fred to confront this one first, by finding a spider and picking it up, using the aforementioned A, R & O theory of fear control.

Accept the fear, recognise that it is adrenalin and a natural feeling, then override the feeling and pick up the spider. Fred has to accept that he has a fear of the spider, recognise the feeling of adrenalin, counter any negative thoughts with positive ones then override the feeling by picking the spider up.

To start with it will not be easy so don't expect it to be, you may well spend half an hour in anticipation during which time you may feel all of the aforementioned bodily reactions to adrenalin, it may even take you weeks or months to summon up the courage. The decision to try is your first victory. By making the decision you have taken control and won your first fight with the inner opponent.

Once Fred has managed to pick up the spider he should put it down and do it again and again until he no longer holds the fear. Once the fear is erased Fred would then progress to the second step on the pyramid and his second least fear, then repeat the process all the way up the pyramid until he reaches the peak.

All of the aforementioned techniques and knowledge should be used in the execution of confrontation.

Sometimes one confrontation maybe enough to deem you completely desensitised to the fear, other times you may have to repeat the confrontation several times. Fred may have to pick the spider up six times before he completely loses his fear of spiders, and yet only one visit to the dentist may see his fear of dentists decimated.

The speed with which you travel through your pyramid of fears depends entirely upon yourself. It took me several years to get to the top of mine, though the overall time matters not, as long as you are working on a day to day basis. As I said before, if you leave it too long between practice sessions the fuel of inspiration may be lost and the subconscious mind may forget the lessons learned from you last victory.

With every fear you erase you will be gaining some degree, large or small, of gained mental strength, desensitisation, exposure to adrenalin and self-discipline. Every step you climb up the pyramid will make you increasingly stronger and give you more control over the inner opponent.

To many, the fears at the bottom of your pyramid, picking up a spider that you hold a fear of or visiting the dentist may seem an eternity away from confronting and controlling the fears at the top of your pyramid. I agree that they do seem poles apart, though, they are not, they are directly related because both scenarios require self-discipline and fear control, though, admittedly sometimes in varying degrees.

The importance of the former is that it actually builds self-discipline and develops a control over fear, which are both pivotal in the extension of the 'cut out' point. Also by confronting minor fears you are getting regular exposure to adrenalin. In theory, picking up a spider when you hold a fear for it, is the same as controlling the fear so evident in a confrontational situation with an assailant, granted, they are at different ends of the 'fear' scale, but that is all that differentiates them.

As, and if, you go further up the pyramid that gap lessens more and more with every step. For instance, on Fred's pyramid, his fear of sparring and confrontational situations are separated by one step, and once he has confronted and erased his fear of sparring there is no longer a gap at all.

Getting past sticking points

THE INNER PYRAMID

It is inevitable that at some stage you may reach a sticking point and no matter what you do or how hard you try you just cannot physically get past it. Whenever I reached a sticking point and I found a fear too great to confront outright I would use an inner pyramid, this allowing me to break the fear down in to smaller, more manageable components, like the 100 mile journey we spoke of earlier in the book. Rather than try to travel the whole hundred miles in one go I broke the journey down into ten sections of ten miles, or even twenty section of 5 miles. We can do the same here using the inner pyramid.

For example, if I had a fear of spiders and could not break the fear in one foul swoop by simply picking up the spider my inner pyramid would look something like this:

Inner Pyramid

PICKING UP THE SPIDER
TOUCHING THE SPIDER WITH THE FINGERS
TOUCHING THE SPIDER WITH AN EXTENSION
WATCHING THE SPIDER CLOSE UP
WATCHING THE SPIDER FROM A DISTANCE
LOOKING AT PICTURES OF SPIDERS

As you can see my inner pyramid allows me to approach my fear in small stages, each stage allowing me build my confidence and gain desensitisation to the fear. En route I will defeat my inner opponent by confronting each section when he tells me that I should or could not. I will also use helper to gain inspiration, read books to gain a better understanding of spiders and prove to my doubting mind that spiders cannot in fact harm you, (there is little point in picking up a deadly spider, nearly everyone would be afraid of such a task and rightfully so) I would also look at worst case scenario and accept that, if the worst should happen I'll handle it. Systematically I will confront one step at a time, being sure not to leave each step until I am completely comfortable with it.

Before you know it you will be holding the spider in your hand without any fear. Then you will be ready to move on to the next step and the next fear.

I will use different examples of how to use the inner pyramid with different fears. This is how I coped with my fear of joining a boxing club.

Inner Pyramid

JOIN A
BOXING CLUB

PUT THE GLOVES
ON WITH A FRIEND

GO AND WATCH A LESSON

WATCH BOXING VIDEOS

TALK TO THOSE IN THE KNOW

Again, if going direct to the fear isn't an option, break it down in to manageable sections. This is how I did it.

I talked to people who knew about boxing and drew inspiration from them, they also told me about the workings of a modern western boxing gym and what I should expect when I joined, I watched as much boxing as I could to desensitise myself to the rigours of contact and to gain an understanding of their strategies, I also copied what I saw in the videos on the punch bag in my garage. I went to watch a boxing class in action, again to aid desensitisation.

It's hard to see clearly what the mind has gotten completely out of focus. Your subconscious mind has a way of making things seem twice as big and scary as they really are, allowing the conscious mind to see the 'real deal' gets rid of any myths that the subconscious mind may has manufactured. Eventually I actually went to the boxing club to train. It was nowhere near as bad as I had envisaged, but then few things are.

As for the fear of humiliation I just told myself that no matter what happened I could handle it, it was worth the risk. Like the friend I spoke of earlier in the book who wanted to get out of a bad, long term relationship, but felt that the world outside of that relationship would be too hostile and unforgiving. To rid himself of the myth he went out and had a good look at what he was letting himself in for. Far from being hostile and unforgiving he found many new friends and experienced happiness for the first time in years.

One of my friends, Jim Brown, is a British champion sky diver. He knows that every time he jumps out of the plane he risks death but to him the pleasure that he gets from skydiving is worth the ultimate risk.

Others feel that taking a business gamble is worth the risk of losing money or even losing everything. Whatever the risk, if you really want something you have to be prepared to handle it.

Rising self esteem

Running parallel with the fear pyramid is your level of rising self esteem. With every fear that you confront and beat, your self esteem will rise and your confidence will grow. You will be better able to handle the things that life throws at you and subsequently be happier without the constant barrage of worries that most live under the dominion of. At the bottom of the scale you are in a position of weakness at the top of the scale a position of power.

Often on the way up the pyramid you will have to overcome hurdles and pitfalls and the road may be rocky, other times the road may be smooth. When you are faced with hurdles and pitfalls overcome them, when you are not don't throw rocks in your own way. I would often reach a high and think, 'this is going far too easily. When is the bubble going to burst?' My inner opponent would manufacture problems to halt my progress. If you are going through a good patch, enjoy it, when you're going through a bad patch handle it.

Rewards

A great incentive for improvement is to give yourself rewards for goals achieved. If you are working on the fear pyramid give yourself a reward for every successful step that you take, even if you are working on the inner pyramid you can, for instance, give yourself a reward for every two steps successfully taken. This will really give you something to go for. Confronting the fear is a reward in itself but because it is intangible it is often difficult to appreciate, so tangible rewards are a good incentive.

Going out for a nice meal, or a night at a show, even having a day off practice might be a good incentive (as long as a day doesn't become a week). Whenever I overcame a difficult task I would make a picnic for me and my lady and go to a local nature park for the morning and really chill out. It might even be an idea to pyramid the rewards with the fears, as you confront bigger fears give yourself bigger rewards. When enthusiasm is low it is often the thought of a nice reward that pulls you through.

Handling distress
Due to the fact that you are constantly confronting new fears and working on the premise that the fear never goes away, the only way to judge your progress is to see how far you have gone as opposed to how you feel. Having said that with each successive, successful confrontation you will become more and more desensitised to the feelings associated with confrontation. Whilst you are getting stronger and stronger you will still feel the effects of adrenalin, or *fight or flight*.

The way of handling the distress caused by the constant exposure is to remember that the feelings will not last forever, they are completely natural and cannot hurt you. Even when you experience it again and again it is not destructive to the body, some people even learn to like the feeling and look for it to give them a buzz. These people are called adrenalin junkies.

If the feeling is becoming stressful remind yourself of these things and again tell yourself 'no matter how bad it gets I can handle it'.

To reassure yourself of these things think back to other times when you felt adrenalin. Probably the worst thing that happened was you felt uncomfortable to the degree that you wanted to get away from the situation that was causing adrenal release. This is due more to ignorance than cowardice. Usually a coward is just someone who does not understand his own bodily reactions to confrontation.

Being a self defence instructor I very often come across people who tell me that they feel like cowards because previously they had ran away from a potentially violent situation. One told me, 'I've been training for twenty years and yet when it (the fight) kicked off I just ran away. I felt so scared. I feel like such a coward'.

He wasn't a coward, he just misread the signs, what his reasoning process saw as 'fear' was really adrenalin, he completely misread his own bodily reactions to conflict.

My friend who was scared of moving to a better job told me, 'I've been working all my life for this opportunity, when it's finally offered to me on a plate I haven't got the guts to go for it.' Again he felt like a coward and that he was letting everyone down. He too misread the signs. The feelings he was experiencing were all natural.

Knowledge dispels fear. Knowledge is all of the aforementioned.

CHAPTER ELEVEN

DEALING WITH KILLJOYS

You know, one of my greatest realisations, and disappointments, with succeeding and growing was when others would not grow with me or they reacted badly to my success.

When I started to experience a degree of success with my writing and had appeared on the television a couple of times many of the people around me began to change for the worse.

A very close friend became abrupt and over critical, even downright rude telling me that no one liked my books and that I should keep my feet on the ground. Another told me emphatically that my first book had nothing but a novelty factor and would never sell outside of my local city. He felt it was his absolute duty to tell me this as though to say, 'who the hell do you think you are trying to become a writer?'

Another associate scoffed when I told him, a little shyly, that I wanted to become a full time writer. He let me know in not so many words that I'd done O.K. (with added emphasis on O.K.) to get one book published but 'don't start getting above your station'. People I hardly knew told my friends, 'Oh yea, Geoff Thompson, you can't speak to him now that he's made it. Who does he think he is?' Even my ex-wife, wife at the time, asked me, 'who the hell do you think you are? Why can't you be happy in the factory like everyone else? People like us don't write books.'

When I told people of my ambitions they told me I was a dreamer, when I succeeded suddenly I became a 'big head'. I can't tell you how disappointed I was with this attitude. For a while there I let them hold me back thinking that maybe they were right. If people tell you often enough (and you listen to them) that you won't make it you start to believe it. They say that you find out who your friends are when you hit the bottom but it is also true that you find out who they are when you reach the top as well.

There can be many reasons for this negativeness, understanding them can help you to cope with and even help the killjoys:

Jealousy
Because your friends wish they could do as well as you they often become jealous.

Envy
Friends often feel envy, again because you have reached a place that they would love to be.

Fear
Close friends and relatives often fear that your success will leave them out in the cold, that you will no longer want them if you 'make it', they show their fear by trying, in any way they can, to hold you back.

Insecurity
The reason why a lot of people do not or will not grow is because they feel secure in their comfort zones, a part of that security comes from the fact that most of their friends and relatives share the same zone, so when you expand and leave that comfort zone it is almost, to their subconscious mind, like you have deserted them.

Resentment

My growth out of the comfort zone caused a lot of resentment, especially from friends and some of my training companions who thought, in some cases knew, that they were as good as me, even though they did not have the bottle or foresight to do anything with their talent. They will have put my success down to pure luck, 'you're lucky that you got a break,' one told me, 'yea, you're right,' I replied sarcastically, 'I was lucky. And do you know the funny thing, the more I practice the luckier I seem to get.' People will give you a million sob stories about how they could have made it if only they got a break. In this world you have to make your own breaks, even the Bible tells us that God helps those who help themselves.

Disorientation

Another reason why people stay in safe zones is because they fear change, change causes disorientation. The sad thing is that if you change and you are an integral part of their comfort zone this will also cause them disorientation. Metaphorically you are standing up in the row boat because you want to move to a better position, this rocks the boat for everyone in the boat so they say 'sit down and don't rock the boat'.

Anger

Your loved ones become angry. Why? Because you're strong now and whilst you still love them they know that you don't need them so much. Once they were your moral crutch, but now that you are mended you don't need a crutch. 'Oh you don't need me now. That wasn't the story last year, you were on the phone to me every day for support.' A little like the walking stick saying, 'oh, that's right, throw me in the cupboard now that your broken leg is healed. Now that you don't need me just throw me out with yesterday's rubbish.' As silly as this may sound this is how many people feel. They fear not being needed, and like the walking stick they feel that they were used.

Part of practice is using crutches to help you expand just as part of succeeding is letting go of the crutches so that you can complete the process. It is very easy to become attached to your crutch (for want of a better expression) and feel that you will never be able to walk without it, if you don't let go of it and try you never will.

So the remedy is to explain to your friends and loved ones that you love then and need them as much as ever but their reticence to let you 'fly the nest' is hampering your growth and causing you to resent them.

Dave was almost at the stage of giving up on one of his friends because of his anger and resentment at Dave's growth and success, when he decided to give it once last try and ask his friend why he was being so negative. Every time that Dave went to see his mate he would make Dave feel guilty and depressed so in the end he started avoiding him, this of course added fuel to the fire, 'Dave never comes around to see me any more. Probably thinks that I'm not good enough for him now that he's doing well.'

Dave doesn't come around to see him any more because he's made to feel like shit.

As a last ditch attempt at keeping the friendship alive Dave rang up his mate and asked to meet him to have a talk about things. Dave confronted his friend about his bad attitude. At first his friend said that he didn't know what he was talking about then said, 'Well, I'm your mate. I'm just trying to keep your feet on the floor, stop you from getting big headed. Someone has to.' Dave told him, 'Look, I'm 40 years old, I don't need anyone to keep my feet on the floor and if my mates can't be a little more supportive with me them what kind of mates are they? Honestly, I'm getting to the stage where I don't want to be in your company any more because you make me feel so depressed.' This came as a shock to Dave's mate who hadn't realised that his constant barrage of put downs was losing him his best mate. Realising this and the fact that he wasn't going to lose Dave as a mate just because of a little success (this was probably the main thing that he was worried about) he made an about turn and he and Dave quickly became close friends again.

The moral of this little, though true, story is, try to understand those who are not growing with you and reassure them. If you can't make them see, very often you cannot, then it is inevitable that you will lose them as friends. They will probably tell everyone that it is all your fault and that you changed and that success went to your head etc. You see it in the papers every day with famous celebrities whose friends and ex loves are claiming that they were deserted as soon as the person became famous. This is part of success and should be dealt with, as usual, by telling yourself that you can handle it.

CHAPTER TWELVE

HURDLES AND PITFALLS

Nothing of any value ever came without a fight.

On the long journey from A to Z you learn an awful lot about B to Y.

There is often a lot more merit in what you learn on the journey than what you find at the journey's end.   G.T.

No matter what it is you are trying to achieve in life, whether it is competence to excellence in the martial arts, faster track times in the world of athletics, building up a successful business, selling, or even maintaining a healthy relationship with your spouse, you are always going to have the hindrance of hurdles and pitfalls.

If there is no adversity there is no advance.   G.T.

The inner opponent, in your own mind, can and will hinder your chances of success in any field, if not taken to task and controlled. The mind can be like an overbearing parent, frightened to give his child too much control.

As soon as you are starting to gain a little competence and get a little way up the mountain of self realisation it (the mind) throws something tangible or intangible in your way to slow you down or stop you completely.

The further you get up that mountain, the more hurdles you climb over and pitfalls you cross, the stronger you become and thus the more control you gain over your own mind. At the top of the mountain is the ultimate goal of complete self-control. On the journey you will have developed, because of your overthrow of the hurdles and pitfalls, an iron will and an indomitable spirit. Also gained would be enlightenment, because in order to get over some of the more difficult hurdles and pitfalls, it is necessary to dissect yourself mentally, admitting and recognising your weaknesses in order to be able to confront and overcome them, and thus, get past whatever stumbling block it is that's holding you back. This mental dissection is what develops enlightenment. This is why hurdles and pitfalls are, in essence, a God send, because without the challenge of them, you wouldn't find enlightenment, you would not develop the iron will that is necessary to confront them nor the indomitable spirit that is developed by never giving in to them when the going gets tough.

The *journey* is, metaphorically speaking, like a bowl of water, you are like an inflated bicycle innertube. You immerse the innertube (yourself), into the water (the journey), to find out, via the bubbles, where there are any leaks (your own weaknesses). Once you have found the leaks you can patch them up. Ultimately, you will have no leaks.

The aforementioned hurdles and pitfalls are or can be many splendoured. They may be tangible or intangible. Sometimes when there are no hurdles imminent, the mind, wishing to abort the journey, will invent silly ones. Basically speaking, hurdles and pitfalls come in three categories, though are uniform in one element, they are all reasons to give in, and are nearly always thrown in when the recipient is just starting to gain some kind of realisation and competence. Recognising them as hurdles and pitfalls and realising that the real benefits to be had from training are gained only by overcoming them, will help immeasurably in your bid to do so.

The three categories of reasons not to continue the metaphoric journey are Tangible, Intangible and Silly reasons.

Tangible Reasons

These are incidental hurdles and pitfalls that are responsible for more 'lay offs' from training than any other reason. Broken bones, torn ligaments, twisted ankles, illnesses (one of my students once missed two months' training because, and I quote, 'Me mum's got to 'ave an 'isterectomy'), the list goes on. With a serious injury it is foolish to keep training as the injury/illness maybe aggravated by your continuance. However, minor injuries should not deter you from conscientious practice. You can quite easily train around such injuries. If your left hand is injured, train your right or vice versa. I was in and out of hospital, and plaster, for two years and had, in that time, two operations for a broken right wrist. I never missed training once and used the time to perfect my left hand techniques. I have also had broken bones all over my body, but still managed to train around my injuries. Training under such adverse conditions requires and develops real will-power and is a great character builder.

With the more serious injury/illness that does lay you off, the danger lies in whether or not you get back to training after your convalescence. From my experience, most people do not. While you are recovering try to visit your training establishment to maintain your ties and enthusiasm, this will greatly help in your re-start program when the obstacle of bad health is removed. A lot of people use their injuries to opt out because they were finding the going getting tough anyway, but remember this, if it was easy everybody and his dog would be walking around with a black belt tied to his waist. If there is no adversity there is no advance.

Intangible Reasons

These can be as destructive in your advancement as the tangibles and in a psychological sense far more painful. Also, because they are mental as opposed to physical, they can quite often by very difficult to admit or detect. The greatest intangible in martial arts is 'physical contact', sparring or getting hit. A great percentage of people leave training because they are frightened of sparring. Even at the boxing club when I was coaching, it was common knowledge that you lost 85% of your new starters after you put them in the ring for the first time. The only way to overcome this fear is to confront it again and again until you become desensitised to it, and take heart, it does get better. The more you practice and put yourself in the firing line the better and more confident you will feel.

Boredom

'It's getting boring.' If I had a penny for every time I've heard this excuse! Boredom is another major pitfall that loses many people from the martial arts arena and in my opinion, it is a lazy excuse. To develop a technique into an instinctive reflex, to develop power, speed, endurance, footwork or anything else worth having for that matter, requires repetition, and what is repetition if it isn't boring? Repetition is practised by the student revising for his doctorate, and paradoxically, by the soldier perfecting a bayonet attack. Swimmers will practice hours and hours a day perfecting a stroke and jugglers will juggle until their hands bleed, all in pursuit of excellence. Boredom is the lazy man's excuse not to practice. You must treat boredom as another challenge, hurdle or pitfall that must be bettered if advancement is to be attained. When boredom sets in you must use concentration to push it back out again. Sheer concentration on the technique you are practising will erode boredom.

Lack of Enjoyment

Lack of enjoyment in practice is brothers with boredom. Another feeble excuse. Enjoyment in practice comes and goes, nobody enjoys it all of the time. The real enjoyment comes from the fruits of training rather than the actual training itself. After all, to become proficient we must push ourselves through the pain of a gruelling training session, who in their right mind enjoys pain, (my profuse apologies to all you masochists out there!).

If you are going through a bad patch of not enjoying your training, stick with it and try to treat the training as a mundane task that has to be done, the enjoyment will return. It's unrealistic to expect enjoyment all the time out of something so physically and mentally demanding, when the enjoyment is there make the best of it, when it isn't cope. It's all part of the character building process.

Lack of Improvement/success

Another favourite excuse for throwing in the towel is, 'I don't seem to be getting any better.' This is one of the mind's best finishers and kills off many students with the suddenness of cyanide tea, after all, what is the point of continuing in training if you're not getting any better? If I may use a metaphor, it is like a propelling spiral that picks up momentum very quickly, just as it seems to be reaching its pinnacle of speed, it starts, or at least it would appear, going backwards. So it is with the martial arts, in the beginning you are learning something new every session and improvement can be as fast as the aforementioned metaphoric spiral. All of a sudden your advancement seems to be slowing down and in some cases you seem, (like the spiral), to be going backward instead of forward, but it is only an illusion. After such a quick advance even a slight decrease in speed may seem like a backward spiral, usually it is only the person himself who sees or thinks he sees this supposed decline, everyone else around him will be seeing his improvement but him.

From my experience and as irony would have it, it is usually the better student who thinks he isn't improving. Every day and every session that you train will bring you, visible or invisible, large or small, some advancement. The child that you see everyday will show no visible change or growth, to the person who only sees the same child every few months, the change is so obvious that they sometimes can't believe it's the same child. And so it is with improvement in training, sometimes it is so gradual that on a day to day basis it is almost un-noticeable, but it will be there.

Silly Reasons

These are the most infuriating and are always employed by people who are using the 'silly excuse' to cover a deeper, more underlying reason or problem, probably one of those in the last category. These are the worst, (and sometimes the funniest) reasons for missing single sessions or even packing in all together, because it means that the person employing the 'silly excuse' cannot come to terms with the real reason.

To my mind this puts him right at the bottom of the proverbial mountain with a long way to go. He'll probably never make it.

Here are my favourite 'silly' reasons, all of which have been used to me, by my own Karate students, over the years.

I can't practice/continue because . . .

1. *My cat died.* (A great excuse because it can be used nine times).

2. *My mother is having a hysterectomy.* (I think he was getting sympathy pains.)

3. *My Karate suit is in the wash.* (As coincidence would have it, the Cup Final coincided with my training time, this was just one of the many excuses used that night.)

4. *I haven't got any money.* (Saw him in the pub drunk later that
night.)

5. *My grandad died.* (Third time this year.)

6. *I had to go to a funeral.* (Hope it's not his grandad again.)

7. *My wife's ill.* (My club is on Wednesdays and Sundays. Coincidentally these are the only days that she gets ill.)

8. *It was raining.* (He must be made of sugar.)

9. *My mum's varicose veins are playing her up.* (What?)

10. *I can't take my grading because my flat's flooded and my daughter fell off her bike.* (The grading wasn't for another 6 weeks.)

Every reason not to continue or confront, with a few exceptions, can be turned into a reason to continue/confront. The real strength to be attained is hidden within the hurdles and pitfalls, if you want that strength then you have to overcome and defeat them.

CHAPTER THIRTEEN

VISUALISATION

Seeing is achieving! Whatever the mind of man can conceive he can achieve.
Samuel Johnson

It's been said that imagination is stronger than will-power and by not trying, by just visualising the goal accomplished it can be easier to achieve in real life.
Takayuki Kubota

Top golfers are unanimous in their praise for it, champion body builders put it 'on par' with diet, and it is used with great success universally by doctors and psychologists, yet it still lies largely in the shadow of disbelief and ignorance. Some sceptics may laugh at the very thought of programming your mind, via visualisation, but who can argue with documented fact (or Tak Kubota for that matter)? I think that visualisation is best summed up by 'Samuels & Samuels.' *What people visualise is what they get, likewise, what they have is a result of what they have visualised.*

Visualisation is a many splendoured thing in that it can be used to attain many things, from building up confidence to perfecting technique to confronting fears. In a documented experiment in America, (one of many putting visualisation to the test), two groups of students were given the task of practising basket-ball penalty shots everyday for a month. One group actually physically practised netting the ball whilst the other group lay on a bed or sat in a chair and, using visualisation, mentally practised netting the ball. At the end of the month both groups met up at a basket-ball court and physically competed to see which of the two could net the most shots. The group that had practised using visualisation won by a considerable margin. That isn't to say that you should replace physical practice with visualisation, but certainly use it as a strong supplement. I have successfully commissioned the use of visualisation on many occasions, and genuinely believe that almost anything is attainable through its conscientious practice.

All we have is a result of what we have thought, Dhamnapada (psychologist).

Many top martial arts competitors are starting to latch onto visualisation and the benefits it can offer. Chuck Norris, in his competition days, used it before he fought and said that many times he scored points on his opponents with the exact moves he had beaten them with, in his mind's eye, only minutes before.

Floro Villabrille, the famous, unbeaten Philippino martial artist who was the victor of countless full contact Escrima and Kali matches practised visualisation whilst he actually trained. He would always go up to the mountains, alone, before a match and in his imagination would fight his opponent over and over again until he felt he couldn't lose. He was quoted as saying, *I can't lose, when I enter the ring nobody can beat me, I already know that man is beaten.*

Before I actually go into the practice methods of visualisation let us first examine what the famous humanistic psychologist, Abraham Moslow, termed the *Jonah Complex*, or in layman's terms, the fear of success.

You maybe surprised to learn that the *Jonah Complex* stifles the advancement of as many people as the fear of failure.

Moslow also stated,
We are generally afraid to become that which we can glimpse in our most perfect moments, under the most perfect conditions, under conditions of greatest courage, we enjoy and even thrill to the God-like possibilities we see in ourselves at such peak moments, and yet, simultaneously, shiver with weakness, awe and fear before the same possibilities.

Many people would, for instance, enjoy the prestige of representing the K.U.G.B. national squad, but how many of those same people, I wonder, would relish the thought of facing the like of Ronnie (the Tasmanian devil) Christopher and others of his ilk at squad meetings once a month? Not so many I think!

Methods of practice
Visual rehearsal, self actualisation, going to the movies or visualisation, call it what you will, the process is basically the same and really quite a simple way of utilising a little more of your *mental muscle*.

Initially, the best way of practising visualisation is lying down in a quiet, darkened room. Close your eyes, breath in and out deeply and relax. Once a relaxed state is acquired try to picture in your mind's eye the goal desired. At first you might find this difficult, but, with practice it will get easier and the mental images clearer.

Picture yourself facing your fears or utilising your game plan in a confrontation, again and again, until it is well and truly programmed into your mind. Try to see the desired goal in as much detail as possible. The brain finds it very difficult to discern between what is imagined and what is actual, all it knows is what is programmed into it, so when you come to perform the goal that you've visualised, the brain gets straight into gear, you've rehearsed it so often it thinks it has done it before.

Many people who already practice visualisation only use one of the senses (imagined senses), i.e. sight, out of the possible five. Psychologists talk of the three out of five rule. Using three out of your five senses, they say, will enhance your visualisation practice. Tom Platze, 'Mr Legs', one of the world's greatest bodybuilders says, and I quote, *If you can use five of your senses in visualisation practice I'm confident that you can triple the results of your visualisation process*. For instance, if you employ the three out of five rule, and as a hypothetical example your desired goal is successfully to employ your chosen game plan in a self defence scenario, imagine the 'feel' of fear within you and confidently, controlling that fear. The 'sight' and 'sound' of your potential attacker before you, the 'sound' of your reticent voice refusing to balk to his threats, and perhaps as a climax see, hear and feel yourself neutralising him with your well practised pre-emptive strike, the sound of his body falling, the 'sound/feel' of your feet running away.

The more real and the more detailed you make your imagined performance the better your results will be.

I often practiced just before I went out to work as a doorman in the nightclubs. I mentally rehearsed techniques that have been successful for me in the past, (it's always easier to visualise something that you have done/experienced before). In this sense I have found its practice an invaluable asset.

Going to the movies

As a final note, if you have trouble visualising images try 'going to the movies'. In your mind's eye imagine a huge cinema screen in front of you, on the screen picture yourself succeeding in your desired goal, confronting the bully, etc. Make the image as vivid as possible, use the three out of five rule and repeat the sequence as often as you can (15 minutes per day) and it will eventually become programmed into your mind. But please remember it is not a substitute, rather an additive to physical training.

CHAPTER FOURTEEN

INTERVIEW 1

PETER MATHEWS

The following verbatim interviews are with a variety of people from different walks of life who have all gone through particularly fearful situations, and lived to tell the tale. Their stories should be used as a source of knowledge and inspiration.

My first interview is with Peter Mathews, who spent just short of ten years in the intelligence corps with the army, and is now a security consultant with a small security firm in London which deals with static security and also teaching and supplying bodyguards.

Q Peter will you please tell us a little about your work in the army?
A The first four years was the normal routine intelligence stuff, the security of the army as well as the combat side of things, knowing your enemy, ie the Soviet army and that sort of thing. I then was posted to a unit in Northern Ireland whose role was to keep a watch on what the bad guys were doing.

Q So that was very covert work?
A Yea. It was a very secretive operation.

Q How old are you now and how old was you when you arrived in Northern Ireland?
A I'm 32 now and was 25 when I arrived in Ireland.

Q Because the work was so covert I guess there must have been a lot of fear involved?
A Em, yes, it's the uncertainty of not knowing what was going to happen around the corner.

Q What was the hardest part of working undercover in such a volatile environment?
A It's the anticipation because you just never know what was going to happen.

Q Like slow secretions of adrenalin?
A Yes, did you see the footage of those two British soldiers that drove in to the funeral cortege, that were killed by some of the mourners at the funeral?

Q Yes I did, was the kind of thing that you, in your unit had to do?
A Yea but the problem with that was those two guys were attached to our unit, they had a limited amount of training, but, you know if that had have been one of us, there would have been a lot more back up and more importantly we wouldn't have been out in the ground that day because we would have known that there was a funeral that day, you forewarn yourself of what's happening.

Q So in your job, the worst case scenario was death? Every day you had to face the possibility of being killed? How did you cope with that kind of constant fear?
A Well you try and disguise the fact that you were scared and also disguise the fact that you were British. You would be sure to grunt if someone asked you a question or if they asked you the time answer by showing your wrist without a watch. If they heard your English accent you could be in trouble.

Q Do you think that the soldiers in the army understood their own bodily reactions to conflict because most people seem to mistake adrenalin, which is a natural reaction to confrontation of any kind, for fear.
A No, I don't think they did. The only way I have come to understand it myself is from coming to your courses. Before that I just put it down to fear, anticipating confrontation and not knowing what was going to happen next.

Q Do you think that you were aware during anticipation of what it was you were actually afraid of?
A No idea at all. We knew who the bad guys were but anything could happen and it was the anticipation of that that made you scared. A classic for instance, we were doing some work and one of our lads got circled by a group of young kids and they just closed in on him, me and another soldier were parallelling in a side street and this guy just shouted out contact! Contact! We ran to where we thought he was but we lost coms (communication) with him, he was being closed in by these four lads, we saw it all happening, and just raced through these four or five guys and ran away with him.

Q So it was 'on top' straight away? Like adrenal dump?
A Yea, it was like, Christ something's wrong here, let's get out of here.

Q Would it be fair to say that you wouldn't have been placed in the deep end like that straight away, there would have been some kind of build up to it?
A Yea, well I was pushed into in quite quickly. I went over there originally as a collator analysing all of the information that was coming in. They were short of opps (operatives) so I got picked and selected as it were, done some limited training and then was out on the ground working.

Q Anticipation, or slow release adrenalin, was obviously the thing that you experienced most. How did you learn to cope with that. Did you just switch off?

A A lot of the time the anticipation was almost excitement, I'd not done anything like it before. You were constantly thinking, I didn't want to let myself down in front of my piers, I'd been given this task and didn't want to let myself down and the people who had selected me for it. At the time I don't think I realised that it was fear, I just got in with it.

Q What about the 'WOW factor' (adrenal dump) the first time you had it how did you react?

A I think the first time the reactions were pretty swift, and then when I analysed it afterwards and thought, Jesus Christ it's happened but I was happy with myself the way I performed.

Q What about aftermath, when you anticipated having to do the same again. How did you handle that?

A I suppose it was worse really, you're more frightened.

Q A lot of people get hit with aftermath and they don't really understand it. A lot of people I've dealt with have an incident and cope well with it but then bottle out after that fact because of aftermath. Again they mistake adrenalin for fear.

A There is always the danger of situations re-occurring, but then it's your drills and your training that click in. You react how you've trained to react, as we teach now on the bodyguard course. The thing was then it was real, it was live, and your life was at stake, it wasn't a play situation, but you never ever got complacent, you always stayed on your guard.

Q Surely that kind of aftermath has to have an effect on the family unit?

A Well, within our own unit there were thirty nine, forty blokes and regularly we'd get a huge buzz by getting pissed and forgetting all about it.

Q And that was your release?

A Yea, there were blokes that didn't drink that much but occasionally we'd all have a good piss up. But also there were incentives there to keep you going.

Q Like rewards?

A Yea. You'd get four or five days off in the main land, the flights would all be paid for and everything.

Q Didn't you find it hard to switch off when you were on leave?

A No, you still were geared up to it and it took twenty-four to forty-eight hours to wind down and then when you landed back in the province you knew you were straight back into it, so there is that couple of days in between where things were nice and relaxed. Invariably you had that mental ability to switch it off and go 'O.K., am I in any danger at the moment? No I shouldn't be'. However you still keep your awareness to a certain level where you're not brain dead but if something does happen then you can move up through your colour codes (codes of awareness).

Q So, to a degree you're constantly switched on.

A Yea, you're not paranoid but you are switched on. I think if you ask anyone if they've got a modicum of professionalism about them they'll all be the same, unless they're going around with their thumbs up their arse all the time.

Q Did you see people around you who couldn't cope with the fear?
A Not really, there were set guidelines for how you were supposed to work. The first time you went out there (Ireland) was a year and a subsequent posting eighteen months and if you did a third tour two years and there was a regular thing with the army psychiatrist to see how people were doing, though the army psychiatrist was never much to go by, it was the old retired brigadier routine. But at the end of the day, you know, it was the buzz of the work because it was real time and was nothing you could experience anywhere else. At someone's decision you could say right, we're going in and people may die as a result of that decision. It was a day to day war where nothing could happen or everything could happen.

Q When times were ugly how did you cope with your inner opponent?
A When things got bad, if the morale was low amongst the lads we would draw off each other. You draw strength from the other guys and they in turn would draw strength from you. It's that team spirit environment. But there were also times when you took yourself away to be by yourself and go through your own thoughts and say 'yea, thats O.K. I can deal with that'.

Q You'd talk to yourself and tell yourself that things were going to be fine and that you could handle the situation?
A Yea, Yea.

Q Whenever I was faced with a situation I would look at worst case scenario and tell myself that if it happened I could handle it.
A Yes, I'd agree with that. You have to accept worst case scenario but it is also important to be positive. If you start getting too negative and thinking that it's all going to go wrong, you'll end up being Neil out of *The Young Ones* (A very negative

student out of a T.V. sitcom). If you're negative and depressive about it you're never going to get on. Another frightening thing is being interviewed by someone with a tape recorder. (laughs)

Q Actually it is frightening isn't it? Why do you think that is?
A I don't know, again I suppose that it is the unexpected, you don't know what question you're gong to be asked, it's not rehearsed, it's the anticipation.

Q I think that there is fear with most things that are new to us.
A Yes there is.

Q How did you deal with killjoys, people in the unit who would try to lower the morale of the other lads?
A Occasionally it was just a quiet chat in the corner.

Q Did you find that as you reached higher positions and expanded yourself that others around you seemed to resent your success?
A There is not a lot that you can do about it, I have always worked on the philosophy that there will always be those who are above you who will shit on you and as you succeed there will always be those who will be jealous of that success. There is not a lot that you can do about it, that is life itself. But I've always said that if there is someone above who wants to shit on me then I'll always try to be good enough at what I do so that he can't do that, but if there are people behind me who are jealous then I'll set my standards and tell them to stop being jealous and do the same themselves.

Q But if they will not grow with you then you leave them behind?
A Yea.

Q I found that as I started to expand and succeed some of my friends seemed to resent me and I couldn't understand because you expect your mates to be pleased when you succeed. But a lot of people just aren't, are they? Perhaps they feel that you are leaving them behind.
A It is the jealousy factor.

Q What was the worst situation that you have found yourself in relating to fear?
A One time we were watching this lump of explosive from the top of a tower block, thirteen floors high with our observation point at the top. Every day we would have to go up in the lift to the O.P. (observation point). For security reasons we would never just go straight to the thirteenth floor, every day we would get off at different floors, maybe the eighth or the ninth and then walk the last few flights by the stairs. Any way, this one day I was travelling up the lift, the lift stopped and the doors opened these three guys just appeared at the doorway in front of me. I thought that was it, I'd been pinged (caught). Their method (the I.R.A.) of operation would be to grab someone, rip his kit off him put him in a boiler suit and a hood, back of a car and then completely out of the area.

Q That would be the last anyone had seen of you?
A Yea. Alive anyway.

Q What happened then?
A I punched this guy out of the way, started to draw the weapon and punched the lift door closed. The lift doors were closing and the weapon was ready to fire. The door shut and I went off. Five minutes later I sat down and was shaking like a leaf.

Q Aftermath?
A Yea.

Q Would that have been your best situation as well?
A Yea, you've had the opportunity, someone has come across you and you've reacted to it positively, like you've been trained to do. If I had hesitated for even one second they could have been all over me.
Q That split second can mean the difference between life and death.
A Yes it can, definitely.

Q As you were exposed to more demanding situations did you draw strength from the victories that lay behind you? I would often use past experience to pull me through a tricky situation, draw inspiration from it if you like. You, know like saying, 'well I coped will all those other situations so I'm sure that I can cope with this'.
A Yes, but I always found that as you get to the top of one tree you are then at the bottom of another, there was always a new challenge. But yes I would draw on past experience and the knowledge gathered there to help me conquer new challenges.

Q I call it the progressive pyramid, when you reach the top of your fear pyramid it progresses on to another, that's all part of expanding.
A Yes, I also used other people as examples to follow, and you'd say well he did it like that and it worked for him, I'll try it like that myself.

Q Do you find that although you dealt with fear in the combat zone that confidence carried you through into civvy street and gave you confidence and standing in things peripheral to the army?
A Oh yea, but it didn't stop you feeling fear, I would still feel it when dealing with new situations but I was able to cope because that's what the army taught me to do. The fear might be getting out of the car to do a cold call as a salesman as opposed to facing a man with a gun but it was a fear nonetheless.

Q What I'm trying to show people with this book Peter is that to be successful in any sphere of life you have to face adversity, because there is a cavernous hole between those who dream and those who take controlled risk. What advice would you offer anyone that wants to overcome fear and lead a braver more prosperous life?
A If the inside of you is scared of doing something, do it, that's the only way. But look at the consequences of what you are going to do and accept them before you do it.

Q Peter, thanks for your time.

INTERVIEW 2

ANDY DAVIS

Andy Davis spent ten years in the Royal Marine Commandos, from the age of seventeen, where he experienced live fire fights as a soldier in the Falklands war and completed three tours of Northern Ireland. He left in 1990 and has been in the close protection industry ever since working as a bodyguard and instructor to bodyguards. He also does a lot of surveillance work.

Q Andy, could you relate to some of the instances you experienced as a Royal Marine which involved fear?
A Yea, I can tell you a classic example of fear and this will make you laugh, my first real experience of fear was when I had to travel down to Southampton as a teenager to take the medical to get in the Marines. That was something that I'd never come across before, and I said that it would make you laugh, the fear of being stripping naked and being examined and this and that, and I shit myself, I was embarrassed and I can remember feeling very scared. I was on the train going down to Southampton from the north of England and I was very nervous.

Q But you still did it.
A Oh yea, definitely. I was already more or less accepted (into the Marines), I knew that my health was alright. But I was sitting on the train thinking 'what am I doing here?' and when I got there I went through the hearing test, the eye test, taking your clothes off and various other things. I experienced all the effects of adrenalin, you know the sweaty palms and shaking legs. Yea, I was very nervous. Obviously it wouldn't bother me now because I'm always taking my bloody clothes off.

Q So it was really the fear of the unknown?
A Yea, it was nothing to do with fighting or shooting or anything like that it was just something that I'd never had to do before.

Q How did you control the inner opponent way back in those early days when you wanted to get off the train and go home?
A In that particular incident Geoff I couldn't really tell you, it was something that I've got that has just got stronger and stronger. But it was definitely brought out in the Royal Marines training, during the training when basically, well it's an old adage and a lot of people say it but it's true, no one in my family thought that I could do it, that inspired me to succeed. I had eight months there (in basic training), it was the hardest eight months that I have ever done, I've never found anything comparable to it since. If we were doing something particularly hard, normally physical, because that is what it is nearly all about, I would wake up really nervous. Like the assault courses, I thought if I drop out I'm out of the Marines, and there was no way I was going to go home and say that I'd failed. That was my thing at the time, I wasn't going to go home and say that I couldn't do it. And that's what I did. I used that to inspire me on. If I had a thirty mile run to do that was my goal.

At that time, it was when being a Royal Marine really did mean something, it was what, a year and a half before the Falklands, in 1981, they weren't that well known, they had a reputation like the Parachute Regiment, and I wanted to be a part of it, I wanted to be one of those hard men, simple as that, that was my light at the end of the tunnel.

Q So you had a definite goal right from the start?
A Oh yea. If you've got nothing to aim for you're always thinking, 'why am I doing this, what's it all for?'

Q I remember reading about a group of people that tried to get in to 23 S.A.S. (T.A.) and it was only the ones who really knew what they wanted from the regiment that got through, the others had no real goal, no road map so when things got a little ugly the inner opponent would click in and ask them, 'why are you doing this, why are you putting yourself through so much pain, what is at the end of this for you?' And because they didn't really know the answers they couldn't fight back and invariably dropped out from selection.
A I think a lot of people are doing it for the wrong reason, same as a lot of people that go on the door. Initially they like the image and all the fame that they think goes with the job but when they get there and find out what it's really about they don't stay there for very long. Unless you know why you're there and have a goal, then you've got something to fight for.

Q They say that success is the best revenge, so if you think that people are expecting you to fail you can use that to fuel the fight. When you struggled in the early days of being a Marine, when you didn't know what it was all about, you controlled your inner opponent by thinking about the people who said you'd fail?
A Yes, without a doubt, but without knowing it. At the time I didn't understand the mechanics of it all, I just knew that I wasn't going to go back to my family and say I couldn't handle it.

Q So you just found a natural solution?
A Yea. I just told myself that I wasn't going to quit.

Q Do you use the same doggedness now when things get ugly or when training gets hard?
A I'll go till I drop.

Q Is that because you've learned to understand and control the inner opponent?
A Yea. And it's (his will) got stronger.

Q Would you say that it got stronger because you've constantly met things head on?
A Yea, I would think so. In fact I can't think of any other way that it would get stronger because as soon as you confront something different, you know it might not be a dangerous thing, it might be like Peter was saying about having a fear of a cold call in sales. I mean I confronted the same kind of thing, what, three years ago when I first started lecturing on the basic selection courses.

Q That can be frightening.
A Up in front of forty people and I'm stood there in a suit, you know and I'm trying to portray this image of being a bodyguard and I was a bag of shit, I was literally a bag of nerves. But then I knew my subject, I'd never lectured before in my life, even when I was in the Marines, I knew the subject matter so I just went ahead and done it. Then after I'd done it a couple of times then you're doing the higher lectures on the week course and teaching on the ranges and it just goes up, but every time there is a another step and when you get there you just think yea, I can do it, you take a deep breath and get on with it.

Q Like the fear pyramid, you're not going from step one to step ten you are gradually climbing the pyramid one step at a time.
A Yes, you're better doing it gradually.

Q And you use each past victory to inspire you through the next steps?
A Yea, you must have done the same yourself, Geoff.

Q Yes, when I've reached sticking points in the past I just tell myself 'you've done it before Geoff you can do it again,' and I remind myself of all my past victories and that they were no different, I got past them I'll get past this.

A Previous victories help to give you faith in yourself. But the thing is, like I said before, there is always something new to confront, anyone who thinks they're at the top of the tree should have good look around them.

Q I call it the progressive pyramid, when you reach the pinnacle of one pyramid you start at the bottom of another. There is always going to be something in life to go for, even though it will be at a much higher level. The feeling of fear does not go away as long as you are expanding and growing, but you do learn to captain and control it. The most important and fundamental factor is that you learn to recognise what the feelings are and why they are there and that they will aid your response to any given instance.

A I think I've got that.

Q Yes you have, that's why you are so determined and so strong because you have it going for you where most people have it going against them. If you could have understood a little more about your own body as a young marine I'm sure that it would have helped you a lot. Many people give in and never reach the full potential in life not because they are cowards rather because they mistake adrenalin for fear.

A I do think though that I have always had that determination, and although I never knew or understood the feelings I wouldn't give in to them, I think it might have been because in the Marines you're taught to act as a unit so you draw off other people and other people draw off you. If for instance you are near or under the governor, whoever he might be, you pick up something from him, you get something off people like that don't you, then as you go on a bit more and build the confidence you become that person or one of those people and people pick it up off you. Then you get a little buzz out of that as well.

Q Going back to the Falklands Andy, what was your worst experience of anticipation, or what I call slow release adrenalin?
A The worst anticipation and slow release adrenalin that I've had was a scenario in Northern Ireland on a particular tour a few years ago, it was the last time that I was out there and I was working in South Armagh. In South Armagh, the particular place that I was in you couldn't go anywhere by vehicle, it was all by helicopter because all the roads were mined etc. So you had to go through the people like Peter (Mathews) who worked under cover, we were informed by them that the I.R.A. had bought two SAM missiles that had been imported into the country. SAM being the surface to air missile which is a hand held thing used with the specific aim to bring the helicopters down. Now this threat went on for about a month I should think, and bearing in mind that you were in a helicopter sometimes six to eight times a day, flying to different places, patrolling, out again in a helicopter and being picked up again. That was a feeling, the same type of thing that you're talking about, but that was slow, over the period of a month. But every time that you went up, and again I wouldn't mistake that for fear, because in a way if it did happen it would happen and there was nothing that you could do about it, it was out of my control. Anyway when you're looking out of a helicopter, especially a Lynx helicopter, for anything that might come your way, not that you could do anything about it, but I think that we all drew off each other then. I was a bit older then, it was about five to six years ago and people looked up to me then and drew off me, and I think you find then that when you know people are, in a way, relying on you or most of the young lads are trying to take something off you that makes

you strong as well, because you can't afford to show any weakness at all, you know what I mean?

Q You've have a position to hold.
A You have to maintain that no matter how you feel. I think in a way some of it is bluff as well, because I'm still feeling scared inside but I can't show it to anyone else.

Q Like the duck syndrome?
A Yea, exactly like that. But that particular situation was definitely a slow release.

Q I don't class any of the situations as fear, per se, I view them as different forms of adrenalin. Sometimes the body will release adrenalin even when you may be just viewing a situation, like witnessing a robbery even though you may not be involved in it directly.
A Well I can compare to that myself, because on that particular tour of Northern Ireland we got six days off to go home and see the family. Myself and my four man team had just come back from our four day leave and were waiting at a particular heliport in South Armagh to fly back from there to our own camp. Whilst we were waiting they (the I.R.A.) shot down the helicopter before mine. They shot it down. They had a flatbed lorry with a point five browning. When they shot the helicopter down we were in what they call the buzzard room which is on the helipad you have like an operations room where they control all the helicopters, and this is the busiest heliport in Europe, the second busiest in the world. We actually listened to it on the radio as it was shot down and I got adrenalin straight away. Not because of the fact that it might have been the helicopter that I was going on because it wasn't intended for us anyway, it was delivering something else, but the fact of listening to someone giving a contact report, the helicopter pilot,

who was the coolest thing I've ever heard in my life, it was like seeing something off Top Gun on the film. As he was spinning and going down the I.R.A. came down off the top of the hill to finish them off. But the army had a reaction team there so they lost no one, purely to the skill of the pilot. But just listening to that gave me an adrenalin rush and I was fifteen miles away, I wasn't even involved.

Q What was the worst situation that you can remember involving fast release adrenalin or adrenal dump?
A I've never had that with anything that ever happened to me in the Marines. I've had it on the door. This was probably due to the fact that we were always in code yellow (a state of anticipation), because we were always anticipating a contact (action) we were never really taken by surprise.

Q Tell us about the door (working as a bouncer).
A We were working in a particular part of Somerset where it was very renowned for being particularly rough, it was just one of those places. I'd been scared on the door there knowing that it was going to kick off (trouble was going to start). As you know yourself an incident had gone off and we were expecting a comeback on that, we were expecting a revenge attack.

Q This would be aftermath?
A Yea, well we were all out of town doormen. We were brought in because the last lot (of doormen) couldn't cope with it (the trouble) but we didn't do any better, and we'd have it (fighting) every night. We'd have the situations with the bats (baseball bats) and everything else . . . and I'd be scared. And now again we are talking about adrenalin and how to control it but in a way, apart from actually looking after myself, I knew that it was going to happen (the fighting) and even though I could

control it in myself I didn't have any control over anything that was going on around me. In my eyes out of the other six doormen two shouldn't have been there anyway and I had no faith in anything behind me, which I found a bit soul destroying when I'm prepared to give them everything that I've got but I knew that I wouldn't get the same back.

Q You can't win in a situation like that unless you've got the right backing from good doormen.
A I never won anything on the door. I've had things that have gone away from there maybe a couple of weeks later maybe when someone has recognised me and that's been a different thing then, and I'm quite happy with that, you know, win or lose because I know that I'll give it everything that I've got. Now, as I say compare that to maybe a fire fight, and again not quoting a particular incident, but we've done, like I say, anticipating it for a month, we're then being shot at and you don't feel anything at all, you get adrenalin but I've never mistaken that for fear and never seen anyone around me mistake that for fear, and I put that down to the training, definitely the training. When you come out of it though and you get, well I won't say shaking, but you know when you've had a good one on the door and you get that parlour of skin and you sit down and you're like that (shows a relieved type of look). And our release is to go out and have a good piss up, you don't drink (points to me) you'd probably go and do a hard session of training to get your release but in the forces we like to blow out by having a few beers. In Ireland you can't do that so it's still in you, because you're not allowed to drink, then I'd train all the time to get it out of me.

Q It has to be released in some way.
A If you keep it there you're going to suffer for that. If you don't release that kind of aftermath it starts affecting the people

around you. As far as training and that goes, and I'm very inconsistent with my training I'll blast it out for a few weeks and then do nothing for a month, but definitely, if I'm not training at home it definitely affects myself and my girlfriend. I don't get nasty-nasty but I'll say things and afterwards I'll think 'why did I say that'. And yet she'll say to me 'why don't you go for a run?' and she knows if I go for a run I always go early in the morning, I'll come back with the nipper (Andy's son) after I've been out for a couple of hours, maybe with the dog and she says, 'oh we're going to have a nice day today,' because I come back, I'll have a shower and I'm like that (smiles happily) 'isn't it a lovely day' all that adrenalin that's been hanging around inside me has gone and I feel great.

Q It gets all the shit out of the system?
A Yea, I always feel better for it.

Q When you found yourself on a state of anticipation what did you do to take your mind of what ever it was that you were anticipating.
A If you think about the kind of situations that I was talking about in the Marines, we were always busy anyway, so we never really had time to dwell on it. They (the officers) always made sure that we had something to do. But also you're that confident with the lads around you and we'd be training, and we'd talk about things like that and we'd joke about it. What I always used to find was just the sarcasm and taking the piss, which is one thing that I never found came across with girlfriends and wives when you speak to them, 'Oh yea, well if they blow us up today you'll get some money out of it,' you know the piss taking thing which you probably did yourself on the door, 'oh we're expecting so and so in tonight I might get beaten to a pulp but, you know, shit happens.' I think that by talking about it, not worrying about it, you can see the difference.

Q Actually having a joke about the worst thing that might happen. So, inadvertently, by using black humour, what you are doing is looking at the worst case scenario and then accepting that you can handle it by joking about it.
A Yea, I suppose so.

Q If you take it too seriously you'll probably fall apart?
A Yea and then you won't be able to do what you are there to do, whether you're on the door or out on patrol, you just can't do it.

Q It seems the same in any environment where there is an element of danger, the door, the army, bodyguarding, you overcome the constant threat with humour.
A I don't personally ever want to work out of this environment, I love it. I may have to but whilst you stay in this line of work you're always going to get that kind of camaraderie that you don't get in any other line of work.

Q I must admit I've been involved in hundreds of fights and yet one of the bravest things that I ever did was leaving the factory, I was so scared to leave because I kept thinking that my whole world was going to fall apart if I don't get another job or if I lose or don't like the new job that I do get.
A I can relate to that Geoff because, although it's not quite the same now, when I left the forces in 1990 you couldn't get a more secure job, I left the securest job you could get in the world. As my time was coming up to leave I was looking for things, applying for jobs and was getting no results at all and I was thinking to myself then, and that was really scary shit. I didn't have the responsibilities that I've got now with the baby and the house but I was leaving a lot of friends and a very close knit environment, you were protected, there was no mortgages, nothing. You get X amount of money a month, travelled the world, didn't have to look for meal or washing, everything was done for you.

Q The ultimate comfort zone really.

A Yea, exactly. Then suddenly it's civvy street. What's in civvy street? I don't know. And I got this job, purely by luck, by chance and then I got into civvy street. But when I was on that I was working on the motorways for what, about 12 months, I earned a lot of money. There was a lot of lads working there as well, but what I found was as well when we're talking about the male environment, the door, the forces, it wasn't the same sense of humour on the roads as I'd known in the forces, they thought I was a nutter, they couldn't get their head round me. They all thought that I was crazy. To me I was just doing, you know, just things for a laugh, not fighting or anything like that, but I really found it hard to relate to sometimes. So what I'm saying there Geoff is that that was frightening, leaving the safe environment of the armed forces, I mean I didn't have to leave, I mean I could have stayed there for another fourteen years.

Q When I started to expand myself and achieve I found that it caused resentment to some of the people around me, did you ever experience this kind of bad feeling?

A To be honest I never, and really I resent the people who resented you, I never experienced that kind of thing. But you're very astute Geoff, you know the main thing as well, all you've done is what they want to do, but they haven't got the bottle or whatever to do it. We both know that don't we?

Q Yea, it's true but by the same count it's very disappointing that people can't be happy for you to do well. You hear of a lot of people saying, 'oh yea, Geoff Thompson's changed since he published that book (Watch My Back), you can't talk to him any more' which is ludicrous, I haven't changed at all.

A I've lost count of the amount of people that have said I've changed since I've left the Marines.

Q Lots of people would like to be doing what you're doing now (bodyguarding) but they haven't got the bottle to even try.

A There are a lot of jealous people about, you can't afford to worry about them.

Q Just going back to the Marines Andy, how did they help you to overcome the fears associated with basic training?

A Well heights have never been a good thing with me, I don't think I'm scared of heights but, I'm wary, and the first time I had to go down the death slide, 180 feet high with all your kit on, bearing in mind that I was only 17 years old, I remember looking down and thinking, 'fucking hell!' I mean people do refuse to go down. I remember thinking 'why am I here?' You can't really explain it and then you just think 'fuck it,' and then you go. Something in my head just says 'deal with it.' My pet hate is ab-sailing and I had a bad experience of that, of breaking a foot coming down the rope. They have a thing called free ab-sailing which is out of a helicopter where you've got nothing to bounce off, all you do is lean out of the helicopter at 90 degrees, look down and off you go. Now I've done that before on the skid of a helicopter and leant out and been really scared. You say again about the difference between fear and adrenalin or them both being the same but I was scared. But again you've got people on the ground who know you and you've got lads who are waiting to go their turn and I know they're thinking the same as me, I know they are, some cope with it better or they bluff it better.

Q Do you take solace in the fact that everyone else is feeling the same?

A Yes, definitely.

Q What about the people that refuse or cannot summon up the courage to go down the death slide or ab-sail from a helicopter?

A I've had lads that have refused the first time and the second but then they've done it and I've got nothing but admiration for them. And bearing in mind what they're thinking then, especially in the Marines when you're doing something like the commando test when they do get a second chance but then they've got a week to think about it and they know that say next Thursday they've got one more chance, but what they do in that week when they know they've got to do something that they've already bottled, and the people that do that then, I mean what do you think of them? What amazing people. Whereas other people have gone for it again and said 'no I can't do it'. And they're out of there, that's them, that's their chance gone, they won't get another one. I always think, like with the death slide for instance, that if I don't do it now I'll be up here again next week so I might as well get it over with now.

Q They say that real power is not in making others do as you want, it is in making yourself do what you want. From experience I have found that the hardest fight has not been with an exterior thing it has been with myself.
A That's the only battle to win in my eyes.

Q Someone asked me once which was my hardest fight, I told them that it was with myself.
A Did you win that one? (laughs)

Q (laughs) I lost a few times in the early days, I have to tell you. but once I had won the internal battle I felt like I could take on the world. What I'm trying to show people though, Andy, is that you don't just arrive in a position of power, there is a lot of hard work involved, and anyone who is willing to take on that work load can achieve the same goals. Anyone can become strong but they have to fight the fight. I've come from a position of weakness and arrived at a position of power, so can everyone else.

A Oh yea, I've got to agree with you.

Q As a conclusion what advice would you offer to people who want to learn to over come their fears?
A All fears seem to be comparable, somebody might find responsibility just as stressful as me going down the death slide, or you fighting so-and-so, we're all in the same position, we're like that 'fucking hell I don't want to be here'.

Q It's true, I can show you a man who has fought four men in a blood and snot fight and yet he couldn't handle the responsibility of a mortgage, it frightened him to death, to the extent that in broke up his marriage.

So whilst the two seem unrelated they are not, they both evoke fear, the difference being that this man could understand the fear involved with fighting four men and could handle it well, but when the same kind of feeling came in the guise of responsibility he didn't know how to fight it, so he succumbed. Realistically if you fight four men you might die, but what's the worst case scenario if you can't pay the mortgage? You're hardly going to end up on the streets, not in this day and age, but even if you did it's got to be better than dying at the hands of four attackers. So what I'm trying to say in a rather long winded way is that if my friend had understood his own bodily reactions to the thought of the responsibility tied to a mortgage and the way to fight it, he'd have handled it. Most people panic through ignorance rather than fear.
A Actually, I can understand that because I have handled fire fights in the Falklands without too much of a problem but one of my biggest fears was on a course here, what, a year ago next month when my girlfriend rang me up and said 'I'm pregnant'. That just totally fucked me up, it was just out of the blue. Bearing in mind that I'd been seeing Kim then for a year, the pregnancy was a pure accident, and I was just scared, I got adrenalin straight away. I said to her 'you're taking the piss

ain't ya?' I said 'no ring me back later I can't talk to ya.' You can ask Peter, I said you won't believe this, and I told him and he started laughing which made me feel loads better (laughs). Again this wasn't any of your fighting and fire fights and things but I was just like that, you know thirty years old, I've always run away from things like that, I've had several girlfriends. It's the fear of responsibility, I like to go out for me beer, I like to do my own thing and I've always liked living by myself and being by myself. And I was just like that, I was scared, the responsibility is there in your face.

I got some advice off Peter C. and then I rang her back and said 'yea, we'll go for it.' That made the whole thing then to hear her response and I've never regretted it since. That was confrontation again, it was adversity.

Q Your final advice for people struggling with adversity, Andy?
A Well all you can do really is confront it, it's like the old adage of speculate to accumulate. But if you're not prepared to do that, and there is always a little bit of risk involved in everything isn't there, whether it is leaving an old job, starting a new job, or going for this or going for that, if they don't want to go for it then they're going to stay exactly where they are now. If you want to go for something just go for it, we've all done that in different degrees. Just step into it. It's like the thing you say, it could be about fighting or just changing your job, what have you got to lose?

Q And the risks are never as great as you think are they?
A Well I always look at the worst scenario, which is what you do, I think that's the best thing to do, and rarely do you come across that anyway, anything in between and you've got a bonus.

Q Andy, thanks for your time.

INTERVIEW 3

PAT LEEMY, PRO BOXING TRAINER.

Pat is a pro boxing trainer who has been in the game for about thirty five years both as amateur and professional. At the moment he is looking after Jim MacDonnell. He has also trained world title holders in the professional arena.

Q Having been an avid boxing fan I have always been aware that in the boxing ring there are no real losers, anyone who steps in to the ring to wage battle with another fighter, to me, is a winner all day long. And there are lessons learned in losing that cannot be learned in any other way, and they are very important lessons. Losing is just another set of experiences.

A Yes, exactly. Life's all about winning and losing Geoff, whether it's your job, whether it's crossing the road, I mean if you get to the other side then you've won, if you get knocked over by a No 79 bus you've lost, it's all about winning and losing.

Q Do you find that it is the same no matter what it is in life that you want to achieve, success in your career, relationship, overcoming fears, etc?

A You only get out of life what you put into it, and that goes whether it be sport, whether it be marriage, whatever it is, older people say that you reap what you sow and that's true. In sport it is exactly the same if you try and cut corners and cheat you fail, and even if you become the champion you've still not really become a champion within yourself.

Q It doesn't necessarily mean a thing does it?

A Nothing. Because you know that you could be that much better. And that's what we all strive to be, the very best of our own ability. As a trainer that's my aim. I see what the guy's got and if he's never gonna be a top class boxer, even though he may think he is a top class fighter, your job then is to go along with him and help him to achieve the very best that he can with his given ability.

Q By achieving your own personal best you have already won, haven't you Pat?
A Exactly.

Q Whether or not that is the world title or an amateur's bout in the local church hall you're already a winner.
A Yes. And then you ask the question of your boxer, why do you want to go down the road, why do you want to go into the ring? Nine times out of ten it is not just about the money it's about getting something out of their life, they might not be the best achievers in regards to academia and they might not be the best kid in the class at school. God moves in mysterious ways, what you may lack in one way is compensated in another and this is why a lot of guys excel in sport, they might not be the brightest guys in the world but they excel in their sport, because they know that God's given them this gift, and it is a gift. I mean you can get to a certain level in sport and you can say yea, this guy's improved but you can get another guy comes along and he never attempted it before and he's a natural, he's been given this gift. It's all about finding that inner part of us, what our pluses are. We already know what our minuses are, we come across them every day of the week, we want to find out what our pluses are. And sometimes it might take a prison sentence where you've got the seclusion and the peace and quiet to know that you can paint.

Q That's the real journey isn't it, finding out what you are really capable of. With people like Jimmy Boyle and John McVicar, both former criminals, it took prison sentences for them to realise their hidden talents for writing. I have found that the reason why most people do not achieve is because they do not dig and find their own treasure trove.

A And you know what, sometimes you may be digging for that crown jewel and find a ruby on the way, in other words, I knew my ability as a boxer, I had say thirty to thirty five amateur fights, never turned professional, I was a pure amateur. I knew the level that I was going to get to and I knew that I wasn't going to get above that. You know, one day I woke up and said 'well look, this is the best that I'm gonna be', I can live with that. And now I look back and I can smile about it because I was, as a young man, probably more honest to myself than most young kids are. So while I was looking for that crown jewel I realised that I had a gift for passing on to others what I had learned. And that's the beauty of this game, you never stop learning, I'm 53 years of age and I feel like I'm just scratching the surface. There is so much out there to learn, like when the Americans came over I learned their approach off them. You can never stop learning. There is so much, and any guy that says he knows it all is a fool, he's a liar and he's a fool.

Q What surprises me Pat is that most people go through their whole life time and learn more about the engine in their cars than about their own bodies and their own bodily reactions to confrontation. They still panic when they feel fear because they don't understand that it is a natural bodily function, and yet they could perhaps tell you what is wrong with a car just by the sound of the engine. That's what this Fear book is pre-dominantly about, teaching people to understand and so subsequently control their own body and mind. How do you deal with a boxer who is suffering with the fear syndrome, Pat?

A What you try and do is you try and prepare them for that day and I don't give a shit who you are everyone feels nerves, it's learning how to control them, that's the art. Controlling the nerves so that it doesn't affect your performance on the night of the fight, and I think the best way of doing that is to do what we're doing now, sit down and talk about it. You can get technical, give them a book to read or let them watch a video and this that and the other, and it will all help, after all knowledge is power, as you said Geoff, but to my mind the best thing that you can do is if you can sit down, and this is where it is important to be able to get close to people, and you might start talking about the weather but gradually the subject will get around to his particular sport or problem, ie. in this case boxing, my sport is boxing, and when the subject does come up and it inevitably turns to how the boxer feels and his insecurities about getting into the ring you explain to him all about the negatives, about how he is going to feel scared and that it is natural. Once you start telling him about all the positive things he's gonna get for stepping into that ring, into his fears if you like, and that will put things into perspective for him. Just the fact that he has talked to you about how he feels makes him feel a hell of a lot better, and how? Because he's probably been carrying it around with him for a long time. Once you start working on the positives he'll start forgetting about the negatives.

So what you want to do is to take him out of this arena where he feels fear and you want to take him into the arena where he feels confident, you also remind him that at all times you must respect the fear and learn to live with it, learn to cope with it and learn to realise that it's that feeling of adrenalin that the body needs. There is only one mechanism that makes the body work at its best and that's fear.

Q So the fighter takes a lot of solace from the fact that you and the other fighters are saying, 'yea, we feel that feeling too, that's natural, that's your strength.'
A Oh yea, definitely.

Q I think that the worst thing is when you don't talk to anyone else about how you feel and then think that you are the only person in the world feeling fear. Jimmy (MacDonnell) was telling me that when he first started in the fight game he was that worried about the fact that he was feeling fear that he wondered whether or not he was cut out for the fight game, then Chris Pyat (world title holder) told him that the feelings he was experiencing were natural and that he had to learn to go with the flow. After that there was no stopping him.
A Nowadays boxers are opening up to each other, you know they've got so much in common they've all tasted victory they've all tasted defeat, sometimes they might have even won the bout but they've lost within themselves, and now they're sharing their experiences. I mean you talk to Nigel Benn, Nigel's first job in boxing was when he had this terrible, I mean an out and out battle, with fear, but when he won that battle he became a different fighter. He even went over to see Herby (Hide; former world heavy weight champ) when he was having the biggest fight of his life with Riddick Bo, he went to Herby's hotel room and sat down with him and said, 'Herby, I know what you're going through, I know how you're feeling, I've been there, I was there last week (When Nigel successfully defended his title against Mcalan), everyone said that I had no chance, everyone said that I was a loser, but I knew, I knew deep down that I could win'. And what Nigel did was sit and talk to Herby and pass on that feeling and that determination to Herby. In that case Herby didn't win the bout but he showed a hell of a lot of courage in defeat. There's not lot of people get up six times, I mean he could have took

the million quid and run after the first knock down but he never, because he was probably thinking, Nigel got put down in the first round, he was out of the fight in the first round, but Nigel being the character that he is and the determination that he showed, went on to win the fight by a K.O. But getting back to the point, this is where boxers can help each other and this is why when I see two boxers talking to each other I'll slip into the background and let them discuss everything because I know that eventually the conversation is going to come back to what they do best, boxing, and therefore they can learn off each other.

You know the old male has always been this guy who wants to create this image of a tough guy who hasn't got any feelings. You know and I know that sometimes when things go wrong and we get home in the solitary of our little bedrooms we all sit down and have a little cry. There is not a man living that hasn't sat down at some time and had a good cry. So when one boxer tells another boxer what he went through whether it was in winning or whether it was in defeat, once they understand these feelings they no longer become a weight on their shoulders, the weight is then lifted because they say 'if someone like Ali can come back from defeat and take the world title for the third time, then so can I come back from defeat, one defeat isn't the end of the world'.

Q I remember Ali as an amateur, he had tremendous problems with fear, the same as Tyson did. Ali's trainer told him that he should always confront those things that he feared.
A Yea, Tyson used to get physically sick before a fight, even ran away a couple of times. But it's the same as anything once you've done it a few times and gained a bit of confidence it gets easier and easier. Not to the stage where you become complacent, you have to always maintain a healthy respect for fear, like fire, like water, respect it. Respect it, control it and don't let it control you.

Q As an experienced man, Pat, what advice would you offer to people in life, not just in boxing, who are failing to achieve because of fear?
A I think the solution is there for everyone, whatever problem they've got in life whether it be an alcoholic, drug addict, or a sports man who's struggling with his fears and that's talk about it, get it out in the open, don't bottle it up, I mean if you bottle it up all it's gonna do is it's gonna eat you away and it will destroy you. There's only one way that you can let go of something and that is to talk about it. Also at some point you have to confront that fear, but talk first, you can't confront it until it is out in the open. Let it out, share it with someone sensible, someone that you can talk to and then confront it. You'll be surprised how the people that you talk to will say 'yea, I've had that feeling, this is how I overcame it'. That really helps, to know that others have felt the same as you.

Q Thanks very much Pat, that was brilliant.
A You're welcome.

INTERVIEW 4

JIM MACDONNELL, PROFESSIONAL BOXER.

Jim was a former double ABA boxing champion (once officially, says Jim laughing, the other he lost on a 'dodgy' decision), Commonwealth Games silver medalist (amateur), United Nations gold medal in Austria.

Professionally, Southern Area champion, undefeated European champion, beat three out of the five world champions that he fought, including Barry McGuigan, and the epic battle with Azumo Nelson. Jim also trains up and coming professional boxers.

Q Jim, how do you deal with pre-fight fear, the anticipation of confrontation?
A Directly before a fight, in the changing room it's a buzz of anticipation, when it's right on you. But, I think before that stage arrives I've already prepared myself by dealing with my friend, which is what I call fear, which I have studied in great detail for many years and have learned to understand that feeling, so I never let it overcome me and I think a lot of fighters who can't handle it (fear) can be world champions in the gym but can't produce it on the night. The reason being, not because they are any less a fighter but they can't deal with the inner opponent. My views are, leading up to the fight, once I'm physically ready, which I normally am two weeks before a fight, I then go to work on the mental side of it, and on the night of the contest I get a bit of anticipation before I get in to the ring but I've dealt with everything else before hand, the walk to the ring, sitting in the changing room, the trainer putting my bandages on, gloving up (putting on the boxing gloves) the introductions, the announcements of the weight, it's all been

done, it's all been rehearsed like a play so consequently when I arrive there (at the stadium) I feel very very cool, very calm and very collected. Even before the biggest fight of my life which was for the world feather weight title I left instructions that I didn't want anyone in the changing room an hour before the fight, at all, no visits, no good luck messages, I just wanted to be on my own to deal with what had to be dealt with, which was the mental side. And I remember Barry Hearn who was promoting the show coming in about twenty minutes before the fight and saying that he thought I must have had water for blood going through my veins because I was so cool, that was the actual statement that he made because he couldn't believe my temperament, but that was because I knew how to deal with the situation.

Q The reason you were so calm was because you had already dealt with the fight before you even entered the ring, with visualisation?
A Yes, that's right. As an amateur I suffered, when I was a younger guy I couldn't understand the feelings that I was feeling, I wondered whether I should be in the fight game. I used to go to fights and I would dread being there. I'd feel great once I got into the ring and box and afterwards I'd feel sensational, but the actual lead up to it I used to hate. Sleepless nights, pain in my lower back, all sorts of things that I now realise are a part of the fear factor, and now I do understand it and I just feel I've graduated in that department.

Q You talked about people that could fight brilliantly in the gym and yet they couldn't deliver the goods on fight night, do you think that this lack of understanding about fear is mostly to blame?
A Yea, I know it's the reason, because I've worked with fighters in the gym who could match me punch for punch but they couldn't perform the same in a pressure situation such as a big

show. Even as an amateur I worked with a guy who they eventually put in the ring to compete against me in the ABA's. The original agreement was that they wouldn't put us in against each other because we were in the same camp and because we were the same weight we sparred against each other.

As good as this lad was in the gym, when it was for real, with little gloves on the fight only went one round, and it was for that reason. And yet in the gym you wouldn't have known who was the better fighter, but I was a stronger person in the mind and I think that was the actual difference when he competed. Professionally you see a lot of guys who go into the sport and everyone thinks that they fall short because when it comes to it, not necessarily at the beginning of their career when it's only 8 rounds and their class gets them through, but when it gets to the higher level when the fight game becomes 80% mental then you get to the situation where they can't deal with the pressure and the only pressure is inside your mind, you're making the pressure inside your own head. In that old statement that Frank Bruno often uses and it's a true statement, if you can't stand the heat get out of the kitchen.

Q You've obviously got to get your conditioning right and have the ability to perform but even with all the talent in the world, if you can't beat the man on the inside then you can't beat the man on the outside.

A Yea. Absolutely. Because I think physical and mental conditioning go hand in hand, part of the preparation for a fight is talking to yourself. I'll explain to myself why I'm doing certain training sessions, when I get out of bed in the morning I've got to say to myself, which I repeat to myself, is that I'm getting out of bed to kick arse, because that's the reason why I'm going out on the road (running).

Q So you're talking to your inner opponent?
A Yea, on a regular basis. One of the things that I do, I did it before the Barry McGuigan fight, people thought it was weird what I wanted to do, but I wanted to be isolated for ten days and I went and stayed up in the Lake District. I checked my own weight, I found a gym that I could work out in. I just wanted to be with myself because I knew on the night of the fight that was exactly what I was going to be, on my own, that was something that I personally wanted to do, and I felt comfortable with it and really, like lived with myself.

Q Could you just enlarge on why you felt you needed solitude?
A I got to the stage where everyone I was meeting in the street was like pulling faces and saying 'you're fighting McGuigan, you've got no chance, silly move,' that kind of thing. All the press was being negative about my chances of winning the fight so I didn't want to read any press leading up to the fight because it was all negative. You've got two departments, you've got negative and you've got positive and I think it depends upon which one you want to build on. I only wanted the positives going into my mind, which is PMA positive mental attitude. But everything that was in the press, which I read after the contest, was derogatory to how I wanted to feel so I didn't bother reading it and like I'd sit down and go through the positives. The positives are 'if you beat Barry McGuigan you're gonna get X amount of money for your next fight, you're gonna go on to fight for the world title and you're gonna have fame, you're gonna have this, you're gonna have that, you're gonna get sponsorship'. The negative side of it was you're going to go back to work, you're gonna be told that you weren't good enough in the first place. I felt like the only way that I could surpass that feeling was to not listen to my mates saying 'you can't do it' I really had to listen to myself saying that I could do it. That's why I wanted to be away from all of the people giving me negative vibes.

Q People are like that aren't they Jim. They are almost willing you to fail. They think that you are pretentious for getting into the ring with someone like McGuigan. They seem to think that you are getting above your station, as they see it. So they try to drag you down by being negative. And when you complain about their attitude they say that they're just tying to keep your feet on the floor. So your way of coping with these people was to simply separate yourself from them?

A Yea, completely, I find in boxing in general you get a lot of people who ain't clued up on the kind of things that we're talking about just now, and that is no disrespect to them, they just don't understand what they're talking about. People said to me before the McGuigan fight 'you've got no chance'. Even before the fight was on the cards people said to me 'I bet you wouldn't like to fight Barry McGuigan'. What a lot of people don't realise is that I had two grand on myself to beat McGuigan at five to two, which is the only fight that I've ever bet on, because, like, my inner confidence was total, absolutely total, and the fight itself was so one sided, I think I'd psyched McGuigan out before we got in the ring. We played a mind game with each other and it got a little bit nasty in the lead up but that's part of the game. Even in the pre-fight interviews when we were told to shake hands for the cameras I deliberately refused on the grounds that I looked at that as a sign of weakness and I wasn't prepared to stand there and do it. It wasn't because I didn't like him as a person it was just a mind game. I was winning and I stuck with it.

Q When we spoke before Jim you were saying that McGuigan was a beaten man before he even got into the ring, you'd beaten his inner opponent with the pre-fight mind games.

A Yea, what happened with McGuigan was I met him at a press conference to announce the fight and we shook hands and he tried to break my hand with a hand shake and from

that day on every time we went to press conference, we had
eleven all together in the lead up to the fight which was a
12000 sell out eventually, there was a needle between us. The
press conference a week before the fight the press asked the
question 'why have you and Maguigan fallen out?' Actually,
come to think of it, two weeks before that at another press
conference I'd told the press that I thought I was going to
knock Maguigan out and end his career and told the press
that they were invited to a party after the fight and that it was
going to be the Barry McGuigan retirement party. McGuigan
really bit the bullet on that one and lost it. He actually
threatened to knock me out there and then, he got restrained
from attacking me, I remember saying 'let him go, let's get it
on'. And I meant it.

A few minutes after that the cameras and the press said,
'this is bad for boxing, fellas, let's just shake hands and and
get a nice photo for the Manchester evening press and for the
TV' and McGuigan actually put his hand out to shake hands,
even then I was playing with my mind inside and I refused
point blank, I said 'I don't wish to shake hands with nobody'
and I pursued with that Geoff right the way through because
we had two or three press conferences after that and when
McGuigan was asked a week before the fight why there was so
much animosity he told them that I'd said something that had
really riled him and he'd never been so grieved and upset by
what someone had said, he said that he didn't want to state
what it was but all that it was Geoff was that I'd threatened to
knock him out and invited the press to his retirement party.
McGuigan said that he was going to teach me to respect a
former world champion and that he was going to be world
champion again, he said that he was in the best shape of his
career he was training with Jimmy Tibbs who he said had
brought the best out in him and that he was fighting better
than ever, he'd had three sparring partners in camp who were

all forced to go home early and that I was gonna go the same way. On the morning of the fight, eight hours before, the press held a conference for a final statement before the fight and McGuigan showed a sign of weakness then, he said that he respected me and that he didn't think it was going to be an easy fight that he wanted to get past me and then he'd look to his future then and that he hadn't underestimated me etc, and then they turned the mike on me and I looked on this as a golden opportunity. The press said, 'Now Jim it's eight to nine hours till the biggest night of your life, how do you feel?'

First of all I overruled the question and said, 'First of all this isn't the biggest night of my life, the biggest night of my life was when I fought a better fighter than Barry McGuigan, Brian Mitchel, for the world title,' and I said, 'I've got no respect for Barry McGuigan at all and I'm gonna go out there and smash him to pieces, I'm gonna do a job on him, I'm gonna show him no mercy and I'm gonna end his career'. And even then I was playing with his mind and I could see it in his eyes. His parting shot to me the week before had been 'I just hope you're there' so consequently when we climbed into the ring on the night I waited patiently for him to arrive, when he actually got in the ring and the ref pulled us together I stuck my head in his face and this is exactly what I said to him, I said, 'I'm facking here', and I repeated it and repeated it until I was told to shut up by the referee. But I could see Geoff that I had definitely won the mind game. And I think out of the forty reporters only one went for me, none of them had seen the inner feeling that he was living with, but I'd seen it early and played on it.

Q Once you'd beaten him mentally he'd got nothing left. Talking about in-fight fear Jim, how did you cope mentally when fighting someone such as Azumo Nelson, and how did you cope with in-fight fear?

A Well I should imagine that everyone deals with it in a different way, my personal formula is to rehearse it, and, I go through things in my mind which I think may happen. I go through all of the positives and negatives, which we've already discussed, this develops the will to win the fight, I rehearse everything from in the changing room before the fight to walking down the aisle to the ring, the music in the background, the crowd cheering, everything. I rehearse what I'll do if things do go wrong, if I get knocked down I'll watch the ref as he counts, I'll get up at eight and walk behind the referee to give me a few more seconds. So I don't really get in-fight fear too much Geoff because I've already dealt with every situation that can happen in the ring weeks before I even get in there. I still get nervous but I don't mind that because that tells me that I'm sharp, I'm ready.

Chris Pyat, who is a good friend of mine who went on to win a world title, when I went to the Commonwealth Games in Brisbane in 1982 we were mates and I was the first lad from the England team to box and at that stage of the game I was, like, so psyched up to win, there were nine of us in the team, I didn't want to be the first one to go out (lose). I was fighting a Zambian who was like one of the tips to win the gold medal and I knew it was a tough draw. I was so eat up and so fired up. I was really in tremendous physical shape and I remember getting in the ring and after the first round I was exhausted, I was really tired. Anyway I won the fight eventually on a 4-1 majority verdict and Pyat said to me after the fight that 'you're too tense, Jim you're just so fired up, you're so psyched up, you're always talking about boxing, you're always thinking about boxing,' he said, 'you've got to learn to switch off'. And that was when I learned what he was saying. The next fight, which was two days later, I deliberately done it. I done exactly what Pyat told me basically. I was against another good opponent who was Ugandan, again a tough, tough fight I got in there and I boxed superb, didn't blow once. And from that day onwards, I think it was like an inner message on how to feel.

Q It's just knowing when to switch on and when to switch off so that you don't waste any energy outside of the fight?
A People say to me 'how can you switch off?' Fighters ask me, 'how can you switch it off when it's constantly there, the nagging thing that is always there?' People say 'I've tried everything, I've gone to the pictures I've watched films, I've done this and that but the fight is still there, you say you just switch off, how can you just switch off?' Again it's self control. I've got a thing, there's a time for work and there's a time for play and I've mastered it because I do literally switch off completely.

Q How do you deal with aftermath?
A I think it becomes a way of life, I set myself to become world champion but I also say to myself, if it goes smoothly that's a plus, but somewhere along that road it ain't all gonna be smooth, there's gonna be bumps, you get cut eyes, you may get knocked out. All sorts of things can happen but at the end of the day I still want to travel the journey so consequently I do all the build up on the positive and the negatives, like you say with the aftermath when the result goes the other way like the Nelson fight then you sort of sit yourself down and you're obviously very disappointed, but you've already dealt with the possibility of defeat beforehand. I think the only fighters that are destroyed by one defeat only get destroyed because they didn't anticipate the possibility of it happening beforehand. They've probably tried to block it out so when it has actually become a reality it knocks them for six and takes all their confidence away.

Q What would you advise people who are struggling with the fear syndrome Jim, not necessarily boxers but anyone in any walk of life?

A I remember Frank Bruno saying to me in 1989, I'd lost to Brian Mitchel in a world title fight, and I felt that my career had hit a level I felt like I needed change, like a player at a football club, I felt like I needed to move on. Barry Hearn was new on the scene in boxing. Everyone at the Royal Oak (a professional boxing stable) had been unhappy with one thing or another along the line, that was Frank Bruno, Mark Kaylor, Charlie Magri, David Dent and I could go through the whole stable. Everyone had spoke about it but not done it, I was actually the first one to leave the stable, they actually called me the pied piper in the end because everyone followed me. I was the one who said, 'I ain't gonna have this I've got to move on'. I had a mortgage and all sorts of things around me that made it hard to take chances. I had to make a decision for me and it was November and my contract ran up to the March but I walked, I went my own way because I wanted to better myself. It was a very sad day when I walked in the gym and shook hands with Barry Mason and Frank Bruno and all the others and they all said to me 'respect'. Because they knew what I was doing, they wanted to go but none of them had stood up and done it. It was the same thing, being positive, even though it was outside of the combat thing it was about PMA, I knew what I wanted and I just went for it. I went with Barry Hearn, who was not well known in the boxing world at that time so everything could quite easily have back fired on me. I was in a position with Terry Lawless where everything was cuddly, I was getting fair money, although I was never happy with what I got for my world title fight, it was paying my mortgage and I was one of the boys as it were.

Q So you had a real comfort zone there?
A Yea, very much so, and in the end I had to go out on my own
and I remember Frank Bruno saying to me 'Jimmy Mac, I
take my hat off to you, I always respected what you done I
wish I had done it three or four years ago'.

I'd ask people to try and be as single minded as me, if it
doesn't work out and it was the wrong decision at least you
can look yourself in the mirror and know that at least I was
big enough to stand up and be counted.

Q Thanks very much Jim.

INTERVIEW 5

ROBIN HORSFALL, FORMER SAS SOLDIER

Robin Edward Horsfall completed grammer school education in 1972. At the age of fifteen he joined HM forces as an infantry junior leader, where he undertook training in leadership and instructional techniques for two years, in preparation to become a future NCO.

At the age of seventeen he joined the parachute regiment. During the following four years he took part in three active service tours of Northern Ireland and achieved the rank of Corporal. He also represented the UK as a member of the Nishan shooting team.

By the age of twenty one he felt the challenges involved were no longer enough and volunteered for, and successfully completed, Special Air Service selection.

During the next six years he served in many theatres including Northern Ireland and the Falkland Islands. He trained as a bodyguard and carried out three six month tours with the counter terrorist team. He was an assault team member at the Iranian embassy siege in 1980.

Robin Horsfall specialised as a para-medic during his time with the SAS setting up and co-ordinating medical programmes in many third world countries. In 1980 he identified a measles epidemic in a remote area of the Omani desert and with the help of the Minister of Health for Oman instituted a inoculation program that saved many lives. He trained in several UK hospitals and is currently qualified as a Registered Emergency Medical Technician. During the closing stages of the Falklands campaign he assisted senior medical staff on the Uganda Hospital ship and was instrumental in several life saving operations.

He was one of only four students who achieved the grade of Sniper Marksman on his Royal Marines Sniper instructors course in 1982.

He has worked throughout the world as a military instructor carrying the rank of Captain and Major in Foreign armies, with responsibility for the administration and training of up to one hundred men. He has trained several special forces groups in unarmed combat.

He has a basic working knowledge of Arabic and German and is colloquial in French and Portuguese.

In November 1984 at the age of 27 he purchased his discharge from HM forces and became a security advisor to the Al Fayed family during the House of Fraser takeover. During the following fifteen months he was a member of a four man team with responsibility for the personal security of the family.

In February 1986 he moved to Sri Lanka and worked as a military instructor in the army officer training school and also operated as chief para-medic close to the war zone.

He returned to the UK in 1986 and became sole proprietor of his own security business which he ran with some success for the next nine months. Although the business had a steady turnover the opportunity to move into diplomatic security arose.

During the next three years he worked as the bodyguard and personal para-medic for three individual foreign diplomats finally operating as second in command of a bodyguard team for the Saudi envoy to Syria who was deeply involved in the Middle East peace plan and hostage negotiations in Lebanon. This man is now the current Prime Minister of Lebanon.

In 1990 he spent eight months as a military adviser with the rank of Major in Mozambique operating initially as a training officer in the south and later as a liaison officer between Makawian forces and Frelimo forces for the protection of the new Malawi-Nacala railway in the north.

In 1992 he worked as the medical officer of Omani gold mines in Guyana. He reorganised the building of the mine medical centre and set up the administration, first aid training and evacuation procedures for the entire work force of 600 men and women. He successfully dealt with two major medical emergencies during his tour of duty.

From 1992 to 1994 he was managing director of Immediate Response Security ltd. He dissolved the company in May 1994.

In 1994 he began teaching Karate full time.

He holds the qualification of third dan black belt in Karate and is registered with the English Karate Governing Body. He has his own clubs in Chiswick, Fulham and Putney in London.

Robin is also the author of *Unleash the Lioness*, a women's guide to fighting off violent attack, published in October 1993.

He is currently a self employed para-medic and Karate instructor.

Q Robin, one of the things that I found particularly interesting about you, in respect to the fact that you have led such a colourful and varied life, was the fact that you said in your self defence book Unleash the lioness *that probably the bravest thing you can remember doing in your lifetime was standing up to a bully as a sixteen year old boy soldier.*

A Yea, I think that's true. You see I was brought up without a father really. I had a step father who married my mother with three kids and my most specific memories of him now, looking back, were of him kicking and beating me, those are the things that stand out most to me. Though I don't hold it against him now. When I joined the army I hadn't had that masculine guidance as I had grown up. So when I joined the army with all these lads who had come from up north and some of the other rougher parts of the country, who were fairly intelligent lads because they had been selected for junior leaders battalion, and the change of characters that I was exposed to was quite dramatic. Very different from the quite place where I had been brought up. I made the mistake of getting a bit physical with one of these lads and leaving and not fighting back. From that point onwards for about fifteen months everyone went for me because I was a soft target, I never really turned around and fought any of them back, I'd back off, walk away and then all the evil dirty little young men's tricks would start, getting darts thrown in your back when you turned around, having your bed turned over in the night, when you were asleep, because you were a victim you were vulnerable. All of this was a big culture shock to me, I'd lived all of my life with people that didn't do those type of things so I'd never seen that side of human nature. I was in an environment that I didn't understand, not knowing what to do in certain circumstances. It took me a long time to figure out I was pushed and pushed and pushed and I got to the point where the worm either turned or you stayed a victim for the rest of its life. Finally this other lad decided that he was going to have a go at me and I just snapped really, I just thought 'Bollocks' I'm not putting up with this any more' and I went for it, and that 'click' in your brain that I'd never experienced before, that kind of 'sod it, well what have I got to lose?' That was at the age of fifteen and it was a big step for me because it meant, right I'm prepared to fight now and I was prepared to accept that I might get my head kicked in.

Q Do you think that that is why most people don't succeed in life and remain victims because they can't force themselves to make that step?
A I think that taking chances is a lot to do with knowledge and education and experience and determination, really it's more down to evaluating the gains and the losses. Big businessmen are not people that gamble, they are people that evaluate the odds then go with the strongest chance; they don't do foolish things.

Q But there is always a risk, and that is what separates dreamers from doers?
A Oh yea. In terms of not succeeding in life, I think that the people that do succeed in life are very often the most insecure people. In a lot of ways I think that special forces soldiers, top businessmen with this driving nature, I think a lot of that aggression and a lot if that drive comes from a desire to prove something either to themselves or to other people. If you take the special forces, the top special forces, as far as I'm concerned, are the SAS guys. The SAS guys are brilliant at achieving things, they are given a task and they will achieve it, they've gone through that selection, that selection process, and you really have to put yourself on the line and beyond it to get through. To want to do that you have to have something inside you saying 'I've got to prove this' and usually when you're a

lad that age you're proving it to yourself because you're very insecure and you go into battle and you're doing the most outrageous things because you want people to see that you're brave, you're super, you're wonderful. So it is, a lot of the time, just a desire to prove something to yourself or to others.

Q When you have the very tangible fear of jumping out of an aeroplane how do you overcome it?
A I think the biggest thing about overcoming fear is knowledge, there's an old RAF regiment saying 'knowledge dispels fear'. And that doesn't just apply to parachuting that applies to everything in life. If you're stood on a nightclub door and someone comes up to you and you are immediately threatened, you are immediately looking at him and using your previous experience or knowledge you think, 'well how is he standing? What has he got in his hands? Is there anybody with him? Is there somebody behind me, where is my back-up?' You take in all of that information and you're starting to evaluate the danger, and as you evaluate the danger and as you look at his build and as you look at his stance and as you look at his hands and as you look at your back-up you realise that the threat is diminishing very very quickly so the fear starts diminishing and the control in your mind starts to increase. When you haven't got any knowledge and when you haven't got any previous experience and when you haven't got any of that big word TRAINING and you're standing there and a guy comes up and is acting aggressively you don't have anything to fall back on and somebody is saying 'right, you're here, deal with it'. What are you gonna do? You could panic, you could freeze, you could over do and hurt someone badly because you don't have any knowledge or any training. The same with parachuting, the first thing they do when they take you parachuting is they show you how the parachute works, they show you how it opens, they show you what it consists of,

what it's made of, they teach you all the emergencies, you go through the drills until eventually when you're dangling through that door on your first parachute jump and all that information is sitting in your head. How many parachutes don't open, what happens if they don't open, there's something I can do I can pull this reserve, all those drills that you've gone through are there. And it's training.

Q And that would apply to any fear Robin?
A Yes.

Q Regarding the Iranian embassy siege, there must have been a tremendous amount of anticipation, how did you learn to cope with that?
A Well yea, because, if I remember rightly we were there for seven days, the siege lasted for seven days and the siege itself went just like a training exercise, like the exercises that we'd previously done. People used to think that there was a set counter terrorist team in the regiment at that time, there wasn't, every squadron, there were four squadrons, every squadron used to do four months and then another squadron would take over, every body was trained in it. It was my second trip on the counter terrorist team and we'd done these exercises where you'd go and sit in this building and you'd do 'immediate action drills' and you'd do this drill and that drill and you'd do getting through windows drills, eventually you'd do an attack and you'd do this option and that option and you attack aeroplanes and you attack buses and you attack buildings and you attack ships, you cover everything. And then eventually one day, there you are waiting to go on another exercise to Scotland and buff, the Iranian Embassy siege starts. I think it was on a Friday afternoon or a Saturday morning and that night we were in the building next door, the Royal College of Surgeons next door to the Iranian embassy on Princess Gate. It was a big day in my life, it really was.

People asked me about it afterwards and said 'it must have been terribly frightening', but it wasn't that frightening. There were fifty-four of us going into the building against eight terrorists so we knew that we were going to win, however, you don't know how many you're going to lose while you're doing that because by the time we actually did the attack we knew that they had hand grenades, we knew they had explosives, they had automatic weapons.

Q Which comes back to knowledge dispelling fear again.
A Yes that's right. We knew where they were in the building, we knew what we had, we'd practised this again and again. When it actually came down to the assault things went wrong. One of the guys absailing down the building, his foot went through the window so we had to initiate the 'go' before we were 100% ready because we were going to blow all the windows and doors at the same time. You probably saw the guys on the balcony putting the charges on, well that was supposed to be a sneaky peaky job and we were going to converge on the terrorists all at once, but of course when you get 'go go go' because the guy's foot went through the window they ran across and jumped back and 'whoom' (simulates the sound of the explosion) and in they go and it was very dramatic. In you go, and it was just like a training drill.

Q What was your job in the Iranian Embassy siege, Robin?
A My job was to stay on the back door and if there seemed to be a break down anywhere we, me and a guy called Ginge Young, were supposed to charge in and support the group that was in trouble. But the communications went down and the AC turned around and sent us in anyway. So we went in and at the time the hostages were just starting to come down the stairs. There are a thousand stories that relate around this but I'm saving them for a book one day (laughs). But er lots of

lovely little personal things, not super hero things but personal things, I'll give you one for instance, a guy called Toad, that was his nick name, and he gets up to the first floor and, there's bullets coming through the door and he had to go along the landing and through this door, and there's bullets coming through it. And all the lads are like 'come on, come on'. And Toad was an old soldier with a lot of experience and he just sat down on the top of the stairs and pulled his gas mask back and said, 'I think we'd better sit here for a minute' and then the bullets stopped coming through the door he pulled his gas mask back over his face and said 'O.K. lets do it.'

The whole job took 7 minutes. Me, I went in at the bottom, the hostages were coming down the stairs and there was a voice at the top of the stairs shouting 'he's a terrorist' and we see this guy coming down. There's me, a guy called Rusty, and a guy called Gerry at the bottom of the stairs and we see the terrorist coming down the stairs and he's got a hand grenade. Nobody can open fire because there are hostages in the field of view, which is all training, everybody knew that they couldn't open fire. Now as he came clear at the bottom of the stairs the three of us let go (shot him). As he dropped the hand grenade just rolled along the floor. We then cleared the building but there were mistakes made, there was a guy stuck on a rope and got burned because he messed up his ab-sailing, the building caught fire, there was one of the officers who was inside the building panicking because of the fire, he was in a real coo. It was my job to stand there and make sure that everyone in front of me was out before I started to move, but he had lost it, so I got hold of him and said 'listen, you get fucking out' and I threw him out towards the door and he went out, I made sure that everyone else was out and then it was my turn. There was two or three people (SAS officers) in the building who acted poorly under pressure. There were two guys down in the cellar who were experienced old soldiers who emptied three magazines of ammunition into nothing, because they were panicking and these were the old and bold. These were the guys that you looked up to and thought 'oh they've done it all before'.

Q So everyone can make mistakes?
A Well it wasn't a mistake, they just didn't have the training, they thought that they knew it all, they'd got to the point in life where they thought they didn't need to learn anything else, and that's a very dangerous stage to get to where you think that you're the bees knees and you can no longer learn anything.

Q So you can never really afford to become complacent.
A That's right.

Q Do you think that applies to most things in life?
A I think it applies to everything in life.

Q Do the SAS do anything specifically on fear management?
A No, not exactly, but a lot of your training is absolutely outrageous.

Q Could you relay any of the things to us?
A Oh yea, sure. When you're in the regiment you are either in mountain troop, air troop, mobility troop or boat troop, now everybody is a paratrooper, but free fallers are jumping (parachuting) at 25000 feet at night with spiralling bundles in the middle and you're trying to fly around them, you know with pitch blackness and oxygen and it was all pretty hairy stuff from 25000 feet. The mountain climbing, I was with the mountain troop and it's amazing how many guys will do free fall but won't go up a rock face. Mountain climbing itself, especially when you're leading, is a unique experience because

it's you against the rock and you make a mistake, you go the wrong way, you get stuck and you'd better have some protection, your skill had better be adequate otherwise you're going to fall and you're going to die.

So you're confronted with fear and you're also confronted with fear in a sense where you've got to be analytical and you've got to realise that you've got to work out what comes next. Like in my book (*Unleash the Lioness*) I talk about being stuck on a rock face one day where I didn't have enough protection, I knew I was on the right route but I couldn't find the next hole and I got into a situation which you should never get into when you're rock climbing, where you can't step back down to the last hole. I was stuck in a position where my wrists were getting cramped, my feet were getting cramped and I was going to fall and I knew it was a long way down. My number two was around the corner, he couldn't see me so even if he tightened the rope I didn't have enough protection to stop me from hitting the rock below. I had a choice, I had to lunge up and hope to find it (a good grip hole) or stand still and fall eventually and hope that my fairy god mother comes along eventually. So I lunged and 'whack' straight into this hole. I made a decision based on the worst case scenario of doing nothing, and this is the worst case scenario of doing something, but actually making yourself do something when at that point you may get it wrong and die is very very hard, but I went and there it was. But if I hadn't have jumped I'd have died anyway, and I knew that, so I made the decision and that decision saved my life.

Q So what they did then was to put you into situations that were as fearful as the combat situations that you were likely to be exposed to?
A Yes, actually I found the simulated situation often more frightening than the real ones. But yes, when we went into a live situation it felt just like a training drill.

Q When you do stints like Northern Ireland how did you cope with that constant anticipation of conflict?

A With long drawn out periods like that you've got a time frame that you're working on and you just have to accept, I think that's the big word acceptance, you have to accept worst case scenario. O.K. I could die. Once you've accepted it you can deal with it. That doesn't mean that you're not frightened, still it it certainly does take the bite away and then you can work at it 100% because you've already told yourself you're prepared to accept worst case scenario.

Q Do you think that this is the universal way of getting a grip on fear, by accepting in your mind the worst thing that can happen?

A I remember reading once that great Samurai would accept death every morning, he would tell himself that today he would die in battle, then he'd accepted that he was going to die so he could operate without fear at 100% efficiency, and if he came out of the battle at the end of the day still alive and with everything intact it was a bonus. It's extreme but it's the same thing and it does work. I remember also a great statement from the JUNE book that I think is very apt and it was 'fear is the mind killer' and it's true, it really is true.

Q Yes, that's brilliant, I'd agree with that.

A I think that the crucial thing if you want to deal with fear is information and training. If you have the information, the knowledge, fear is often completely dispelled and if it isn't you can deal with it with the training.

Q Finally, Robin, what advice would you offer people who may be struggling with the fear syndrome, not necessarily in a combat sense but any kind of adversity?

A Whatever it is you're frightened of, train yourself or get training to deal with it, to understand it. To be able to overcome a fear you've got to understand that fear, the more you understand about the thing that is threatening you the less of a threat it becomes and the less dangerous it becomes. Eventually, the more you understand it, it almost goes away and very often you realise that there was no real danger there in the first place and that it wasn't anything to worry about. You want to do a bungy jump go and study bungy jumping, understand what the rope is made of, understand how high the crane goes, understand the pressures and the pounds per square inch and everything that goes into it, then you go and do it because all of a sudden it is no longer that scary. First study it and then confront it, if you feel that you need to confront it, after you have studied it you may no longer have to confront it because the fear may be completely dispelled so you no longer have to prove anything because you are not scared of it any more.

Q Robin, thanks very much for you time.

EPILOGUE

As I have said throughout the book, admit your fears, learn to understand them and then systematically confront them one by one until they have all been dispelled. Expect adversity, that is the price you may have to pay for a braver life, but it will be worth it. I wish you, whoever you may be, the very best of luck with your endeavours.